The
Sacrament

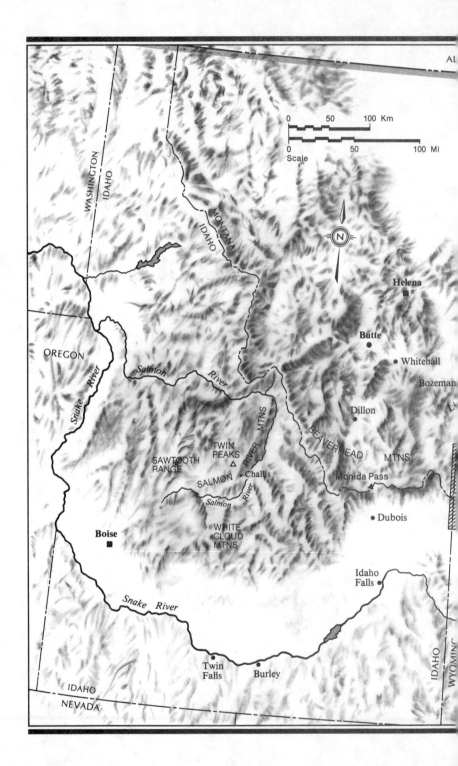

AL

WASHINGTON

IDAHO

0   50   100 Km

0   50   100 Mi
Scale

MONTANA

IDAHO

N

Helena

OREGON

Butte

Salmon   River

Whitehall

Bozeman

Snake   River

Dillon

Li

RIVER MTNS

TWIN
PEAKS
△

BEAVERHEAD   MTNS

SAWTOOTH
RANGE

SALMON

Challis

Monida Pass

Salmon   River

Boise

WHITE
CLOUD
MTNS

Dubois

Idaho
Falls

Snake   River

IDAHO

WYOMING

Twin
Falls

Burley

IDAHO

NEVADA

SASKATCHEWAN

CANADA

Estevan •

UNITED STATES

MONTANA

NORTH
DAKOTA

• Williston

The Sacrament

Peter Gzowski

ne

McCLELLAND AND STEWART

J. Loates

Copyright © 1980 by McClelland and Stewart Limited

ALL RIGHTS RESERVED

The Canadian Publishers
McClelland and Stewart Limited
25 Hollinger Road, Toronto M4B 3G2

Published simultaneously in the United States by
Atheneum Publishers.

Map by James Loates

Photographs by:
National Transportation Safety Board, Washington, D.C.
(pages 9 and 31)
Peter Ng, *The Estevan Mercury* (page 175)

CANADIAN CATALOGUING IN PUBLICATION DATA

Gzowski, Peter.
  The sacrament

ISBN 0-7710-3738-4

1. Survival (after airplane accidents, shipwrecks,
etc.). 2. Aeronautics – Idaho – Accidents – 1979.
3. Cannibalism. I. Title.

TL553.7.G96 979.6'72033'0922 C80-094535-2

Printed in the United States of America

Contents

"I'm going to tell you a story that when you first listen to it you swear it would be a tragedy with a little mixed happiness. But it isn't. The whole story is nothing short of a modern miracle."

—Brent Dyer, May 29, 1979

I
The Crash
May 5, 1979

Chapter One

Spring came late to the high country of the western American cordillera in 1979, and on the afternoon of May 5, when a small white aircraft flew westward from the Montana prairie toward the mountains that reach into central Idaho, snow was gusting through the air. Darkness threatened. The snow scudded out of banks of cumuliform clouds above the mountain ranges and blew stiffly into the aircraft's nose. It obscured the call letters set into the black racing stripes along the plane's fuselage – C (for Canada)-GYVP – and the proud gold trademark on its swept-back tail, the Skyhawk.

The little plane was struggling. Ice was forming on the leading edges of its wings and on the fairings of its wheel assembly. The ice added to the Skyhawk's already heavy load and violated the aerodynamics of its design.

Under gentler circumstances the plane would have soared easily above the peaks that lay ahead. The Skyhawk was a Cessna 172, and the Cessna is the most popular single-engined aircraft in the world, a Volkswagen of the American air. One of the reasons for its popularity is its safety; it is strong and efficient, and manoeuvrable. If the Cessna 172 has a weakness, it is in its very dependability; pilots sometimes rely on it too much. The more familiar they become with the plane, the more confident they grow that it will make up for their mistakes and deliver them from their own errors in judgement. Aviation people call this phenomenon "contemptuous familiarity." That day, when the circumstances were far from gentle, with a full load of fuel picked up at their last stop less than an hour before at Livingston, Montana, and with four adults strapped into the confines of its tiny cabin, GYVP was being tested to its limit.

The landscape ahead was awesome. The high country of the cordillera includes some of the most rugged terrain in America. On maps the ranges into which the plane was headed are clearly delineated by name: the Sawtooths, the Boulders, the Salmon River, the White Clouds. But from the air they appeared as one continuous wilderness. On the horizon, the downward line of one slope ran into the upward thrust of the next peak, then dipped again into a gentle valley, only to lift again toward the sky.

Even the few people who know the mountains well have difficulty distinguishing them by name. The Alps of America, these ranges are called. Dozens of their summits reach over 11,000 feet, not much below the majesty of the Rockies, into which they eventually merge. In summer, when the sun illuminates the pink, blue, purple, and brown pastels of their facets, the mountains are staggeringly beautiful. Long before white men began to claw at the minerals in their rocks, the Indians would gaze on them with wonder. Sometimes, in the summer, the Nez Perce, the Shoshone, or the Bannock would pursue the big-horn sheep, the ahsanti, into the heights of the mountains. But in the winter, when the colours turned to monochromes of snow and ice and bare granite, even the Indians shunned the peaks. The mountains of Idaho are fierce and terrible, and they have repelled all but the hardiest settlers. They remain primeval. Pilots who fly in the air that twists and lurches above them respect and fear its currents as the sailor respects and fears the forces of the sea.

At the controls of the Cessna, Norm Pischke fought for altitude. His lips were tight, but he might well have been grinning to himself. He was a laconic man in the most trying of times, known for his slow temper and his quiet manner. Flying gave him all the thrills he seemed to need, and to some of the people who called themselves his friends, it sometimes appeared that danger exhilarated him: the greater the risks, the more heightened his joy. He was a big man, more than 200 pounds. Now, the muscles of his neck were taut above the fold of his turtleneck sweater, and his shoulders bulged under his leather jacket. For all the tension in the cabin, he seemed at ease. The laces on his shoes, resting on the rudder pedals, were undone. The glasses he needed occasionally bounced on the dashboard ahead of him, beside his wallet, still open at the celluloid-enclosed credit card he'd used to buy their load of fuel. The Cessna was his, the flagship of his small charter business in Estevan, Saskatchewan, a business that was the fulfilment of his twenty years of flying and more than 6,000 hours in the air. He was in his element.

Air is liquid, mountain pilots like to say. Aircraft are afloat in it. It rolls up the windward side of the slopes and crashes surf-like over the top. Roaring through the crags and valleys, the wind stirs and rear-ranges the patterns of temperature that have caused it to blow in the first place. Wind begets wind. Updrafts lift. Side-drafts buffet. Downdrafts press like the hands of God.

The Cessna was refusing to climb. Its Lycoming engine, whining in its struggle to suck enough oxygen from the air to feed its 160 horses, could barely hold the plane at 10,000 feet, well below the height of the mountains ahead. With a lesser load, and in still air at sea level, the Cessna can climb 770 feet a minute, up to 14,000 feet and above, but with the force of a strong downdraft adding to its weight in the thin mountain air, GYVP was losing both altitude and headway. The snow and the wind were growing worse.

As forward momentum decreased, the plane began to lose the vac-uum behind the trailing edges of its wings. Without vacuum, the reeds of the stall-horns sounded their alarm. The squeal in the cabin warned that the craft was within five knots of airspeed of tumbling out of control.

In the co-pilot's seat on Norm's left, Brent Dyer turned to speak.

"Should those things be going off?" he asked. His thin young voice strained against the squawking horns.

"Just back-pressure from the mountains," Norm shouted. "Doesn't mean a thing."

Earlier in the trip Brent had flown the plane himself, using the second set of controls – the learner's set. Brent, the son of an Estevan car dealer, was one of Norm's better student pilots. One of the pur-poses of the trip had been to log some cross-country hours toward his licence. He'd taken the Cessna off from Estevan that morning and had landed it at each of the two stops along the way, once in North Dakota and again in Livingston, Montana, and he'd chortled with pride at each achievement.

Brent was a cocky young man, certain of his own abilities. Norm had noticed his confidence when he'd first walked into the Norm Air hangar-office the previous fall. He was curly haired and wiry, with a funny way of looking at you. Quizzical, he seemed to sniff the air like a prairie gopher. Norm had confidence in Brent, and when the other passengers had wondered about having a twenty-five-year-old neophyte at the controls as the weather started to threaten on the way into the mountains, he had endorsed his student. "Listen," he had said, "you could turn this thing upside down in the middle of the night and Brent would know where he was. He's got the best built-in sense of direction of anyone I've ever met."

In the back seat, Don Johnson had chuckled over that one. Don was Brent's father-in-law. A successful businessman, the Kentucky Fried Chicken King of southeast Saskatchewan, he was picking up the tab for the trip. He remembered a holiday the family had taken the winter before, up to Uranium City in northern Saskatchewan, to do some hunting and snowmobiling. They'd been visiting Don's brother, Keith, a mining executive whom Brent hadn't met before. A bunch of them had strayed on their snowmobiles, and for a while they'd lost their bearings. But Brent had just let out a whoop – "Follow me!" – and roared off over the nearest rise. Sure enough he'd taken them directly back to Keith's house for steaks and hot chocolate.

Brent didn't drink. Not any more. Not for the seven years since he'd joined Alcoholics Anonymous. He'd been a heller of a kid, in constant trouble around Estevan, and when he was eighteen, not long after he'd married Don's oldest daughter, Cindy, the troubles had come to a head. He'd been caught breaking into a gas station for money to buy booze and had been sent to the Regina Correctional Institute. After that – not *right* after it, but not much later – he'd straightened up, and now here he was all gussied up in his cord jacket, neat as a headwaiter, peering ahead through the windshield with that curious alert expression he often had when things were happening around him.

"Too bad cars don't have dual controls," Don said. "You could switch off driving without having to stop."

Cars were a part of Don's life as airplanes were not. He drove everywhere, dashing off on the flimsiest of excuses in his grey Lincoln to visit one of his chain of restaurants, eight of them now, stretching from Moosomin in the north down to Williston, North Dakota. He seemed always to be on the move, and Norm and Brent had figured that if the trip went well Don might be interested in flying more for business, either chartering from Norm or buying a small aircraft for himself. Earlier in the flight they'd talked about it. Don had wondered if, at fifty, he wasn't too old to fly.

"Hell," Norm said, "there's a guy who comes out to the airport for lessons and he's seventy-five."

"There'll be some real good second-hand Mooneys at Boise," Brent had said.

Boise, still 200 miles away, was their destination. The third and most important reason for the trip was to pick up the dog that should be waiting for them now at the Boise airport. The dog, a West Highland White Terrier pup, was a present for Donna, Don's seventeen-year-old daughter and the younger sister of Brent's wife.

Donna was sitting quietly in the back seat now, beside her father, almost touching him, idly playing with a curl in her long blonde hair. She hadn't been talking much. She didn't want to be late getting to Boise. She'd been looking forward to seeing the Westie pup for too long. Now, she wanted only to pick up the dog and, after a good night's sleep, fly back to Estevan to show the pup to her boyfriend Ron on Sunday, before they had to go to school again. Maybe she shouldn't have come at all. She was supposed to have given a baton class today. This was the first time she hadn't shown up for baton this year. When would they get to Boise? she wondered. Weren't the others as scared as she was?

The trip had seemed so simple that morning. Brent was the first one up. Waking early wasn't unusual for Brent, who, like a lot of reformed alcoholics, had trouble sleeping late in the mornings. Often before he went to work at his father's car lot he would rise to feed his two young sons, and horse around a while with them before Cindy got up. He enjoyed the early sounds around their comfortable bungalow. And he enjoyed his noisy, tow-headed boys: Geoffrey, aged seven, and little Jay, four. Even after seven years as a married man, he still revelled in being the master of his own house. Morning was the best time to play his role, before he jumped in whatever car he was borrowing from the lot that day, or into his own four-wheeled drive land vehicle, and drove the few blocks to Dyer Ford.

But today he'd been more restless than usual, kicking off the covers before the grey of the morning peeked through the bedroom curtains. He reached over Cindy for the bedside phone and dialled the Johnson's number.

Donna, who'd been dreaming of her new dog, rushed down to the living room to answer the phone.

"Anyone up?" Brent said. Even first thing in the morning you could hear the energy in his voice.

"Dad's not awake yet."

"Tell him to get going. Rise and shine."

"Brent, the weather looks awful."

"I'll call Norm at the airport."

The phone had also wakened Donna's father. He came downstairs rubbing his chin, looking for coffee.

"Was that Brent?" he asked.

"He's just going to call Norm."

"We going?"

"I guess so."

"Don't forget your bathing suit."

She would have, too. She'd forgotten there'd be a pool at the motel in Boise. That was like her dad, remembering that kind of detail – just the kind of thing she knew he did in his business, because sometimes he'd bring some of the books home and show her how they worked. He always thought of the details.

There was little Don Johnson would not have done for Donna. The rest of the family, especially Cindy and their older brother Brian, sometimes teased them about their relationship. "You're really a spoiled brat," Cindy had said once to Donna. But Don and Donna could laugh at the teasing; they knew the others didn't really mean it. It was as if Don, who took so much pleasure from all three of his offspring, was determined to draw out the time he had with his youngest, to enjoy her childhood as long as he could.

He was good to all his children; no matter how hard he was working he always found time for them and he took them along on as many business trips as he could. Each had received a car as a sixteenth birthday present, although – and this was typical of him – he insisted they act with what he called responsibility in return. He stood by all of them. No matter how he'd felt about Cindy's early marriage to Brent, he'd supported her. Brian, now with his degree in business administration, was fitting nicely into the business, and one could sense Don's pride in him. But there was never any doubt in anyone's mind that Donna was his favourite. Only last week, Evelyn, Don's strong and quiet wife, had mentioned his special treatment of their youngest. "You're going to ruin her," she'd said. "Oh, I don't think so," he'd answered, and then smiled. "Anyway, what if I do?"

Right from the time Donna had been brought home from the hospital, her father had special names for her. She was his "butterball." Then, just "the kid." "Where's the kid?" he would say each night when he got home, and she would run to him to see – especially when he'd been out of town – what new treat he had brought for her. As she grew through chubby childhood and into the blonde, innocent beauty of adolescence, he would wait up for her when she was out in the evenings. Once, when he got home from work tired, he found her in tears in the living room. What was the matter? It was raining, she said, and she had an appointment to have her hair done. He drove her downtown and waited so he could drive her home in comfort. He took her once on a shopping trip of her own to Minneapolis. She loved to shop; he loved to take her. When she took up baton-twirling, he was as proud of her accomplishments and awards as he was of his own increasing success in business. When Colonel Saunders himself had come to Estevan, Don had introduced her as "my daughter the majorette." The colonel had beamed.

The family was Don's life. Time that other men he knew gave to hunting or fishing or just being "out with the boys" he gave to his kids. The things he delighted in buying – the cars, the piano, even the van they had just finished having customized – were family possessions, not personal ones. Yet sometimes it seemed that these material things made up for his inability to express his love more directly. He was not a physically demonstrative man. He did not kiss or hug freely. Even when the children were little, and he had to leave them for a business trip, he would line them up by the door, and then move down the line like an officer reviewing his troops, shaking hands with each of them in formal farewell.

Brent telephoned again before Donna finished her milk – she never could stand coffee – to say that Norm didn't like the weather at the moment, but he thought in another hour or so they could leave. He'd get some more information, but they should count on going. The Johnsons relaxed over breakfast and talked about the Westie, how Donna would look after it. She took out the snapshots its breeder had sent her, to have one more look before they left.

With little luggage, just a leather Bauer carrying bag each for Brent and Donna, and Don's usual Samsonite suitcase, they decided to take Donna's Bobcat to the airport. Brent had a couple of things he wanted to do at his father's car lot, and Donna went around the corner to Hender's Drugs to pick up some snacks for the trip. What she really wanted was some pop, but her mother had reminded her there'd be no washroom in the small plane and she shouldn't drink much. She bought little.

Sharon Pischke, Norm's wife, was in the airport office when they got there. A pretty woman in jeans and a T-shirt, she was talking to Norm with her hands stuck in her hip pockets. Brent, acting the host, introduced everyone, and Norm welcomed them all aboard. Donna was a little surprised that her father hadn't met Norm before; he knew nearly everyone else in Estevan. Norm seemed like a nice man, strong and capable. He said they could take off as soon as they were ready. There was some heavy weather down south, but he was pretty sure it would clear. Don tried to phone Idaho to say they were running a bit late, but he couldn't get through.

Donna, Don, Brent, and Norm left the office of Norm Air together, and started to walk across the runway.

"It's pretty small, isn't it?" Donna said.

Brent laughed.

"What's so funny?"

"You think that's small, eh?"

"Sure. Why?"

"You're looking at the wrong plane. That's Jumbo Panteluk's twin-engine Aztec. It's worth about two hundred thousand bucks."

"And that's not ours?"

"No. That one there. That's Norm's – the Cessna 172."

It was *tiny*; she felt as if she should pet it. Perched on its front wheels, with its nose pointing in the air, it reminded her of a small animal begging to be taken on an outing. It was hardly bigger than her Bobcat. The luggage compartment where Norm and Brent put the bags, opening off the fuselage from just behind the left-hand door, seemed even smaller than the car's trunk. She had to duck her head under the wing and hunch down to get into the cabin. Tilting one of the front seats forward, Donna slid into the rear seat. When she leaned back to fasten her seatbelt, she realized there was less than a foot of space behind her head.

Donna sat on the right, behind Norm, who needed to slide his chair back to its fullest extension. Her dad was on her left, where there was extra legroom in the space behind Brent. Each of them had a window, but it wasn't like flying in the commercial airliners she'd been in before.

In the co-pilot's seat, Brent poured the last of the coffee out of the Thermos. God, he could go through coffee. That and Cokes – ever since he'd stopped drinking. He'd have himself some Cokes tonight, when they got to Boise. Let the other men have their beers. He could get along without them if he wanted. Like all AA's, he just got through one day at a time. Sometimes he wondered what it would be like to get drunk again, but he never really felt the urge. Well, maybe when other people around him were drinking, but he knew how bad he could get, and he was proud of the way he'd straightened out. That had shown a few people.

The drinking had started early. Sometimes he himself couldn't believe how young he'd been. When he was eight, he broke into his father's liquor cabinet and helped himself to a shot of rye. Unlike most kids (he'd learned later), he liked it. That was hardly the start of his serious drinking, but it didn't take him long. By the time his voice changed he was a regular boozer – Friday night outings onto the prairie in someone's car, or dipping into the stock of whoever's parents were out for the evening. By his mid-teens, he was a practising alcoholic. Maybe he was born with it. Maybe even inherited it. He'd heard that his grandfather Jack had been a pretty good drinker.

Jack Dyer was the son of a remittance man; he'd come to Estevan in the twenties to help set up the new electric power plant. Estevan in those days was a wide open saloon town, right on the Soo Line that ran down to the States. Bootlegging had been big business when the U.S. went dry. There were whole stills under the waters of the lake at Boundary Dam, Brent had heard, and someday maybe he'd go looking for them when he was scuba diving. Anyway, Jack had apparently been a popular patron of the local bars, and kept it up long after he'd left his wife and Brent's father, Jimmy, on their own while he went off to seek his fortune in the North. Jimmy still didn't like to talk about Jack; he hadn't even gone to the old man's funeral a couple of years ago out on the coast. But he did admit Brent had a lot of his grandfather's skills around mechanical things – there were few devices Brent couldn't take apart and put back together the first time he saw them – and maybe he'd got his liking for liquor from the same set of genes.

What did it matter? He was an alcoholic, just as he testified at AA meetings and just as he emphasized in the talks he sometimes gave to young people around town. He didn't have that craving in the mornings you read about in the AA literature, but almost everything else. Blackouts? Christ, he couldn't remember half the things he'd done when he was tanked up, and sometimes when the cops came after him for some trouble the night before he didn't even know what they were talking about. It was the booze that got him in trouble – the break-ins and stuff. Luckily, he'd never been caught drunk at the wheel of a car, although even without booze he'd had enough trouble in the cars his dad let him borrow.

Brent had always been small for his age, but he'd made a lot of friends who could get him something to drink, and even in the sixties, when he was growing up, there was always a bootlegger who didn't care about the customer's age. Having a car helped too, and Jimmy, who'd built up a good Ford dealership after the war, had never stinted on making sure Brent had wheels. He'd got his first car when he was sixteen, and not long after that his first ticket. The violations piled up: speeding, driving "without due care and caution," and one for obscene language when he drove through the window of a local store. The guy's wife had tried to take his keys away and he'd told her to . . . . Well, hadn't she heard that word in a movie? He'd wanted his lawyer to ask the judge that question.

He took great delight in his own cleverness. One of his favourite cars was a '68 Mustang whose windshield fluid was activated by a foot-pedal. Brent filled the fluid container with Seagram's Crown Royal – made by the same Bronfman family that used to sell booze around Estevan, or so he'd heard – and ran a hose under the dashboard, so he could pour himself a shot while he was driving along. "Want a double?" he'd ask his friends. "That's two pumps of the pedal."

And he was sly. When he decided early in his high-school career that French didn't appeal to him – he found most school subjects pretty easy but he never worked at any of them, and his marks were no measure of his intelligence – he made the appropriate appeal to the teacher, who agreed that his dropping French would be a good idea. Then he neglected to tell the principal's office. He found himself with an unofficial extra spare period each day since the teacher, not expecting him, wasn't marking him absent. He devoted this extra time to improving his pool game. Pool was one of the few competitive activities he enjoyed. The common boyhood sports of the prairie – most notably, of course, hockey – held little appeal for him. He was, in spite of all his friends, a loner. The only competition he enjoyed was against himself, testing his own abilities.

At every opportunity he haunted the prairie – the vast, empty, open, wild land that was so much a part of the town and the town's way of life. The prairie was his turf. He liked to pick mushrooms in the spring. In the summers, often by himself, he would hike to the spring-fed lakes among the spill-piles of the Estevan coal fields to stalk rainbow trout. He could spend hours there, by himself, staring into the dark water and watching the fish play in the shadows of the sky. But he liked to catch them too, and bring them home for supper. He was good, even expert, with guns. He loved guns. Jimmy gave him his first shotgun when he was just a kid. He would shoot tin cans for practice, gophers for fun, ducks, geese, and pheasants for meat. In the fall, when the deer were abundant on the fields of southern Saskatchewan, Brent would watch contemptuously as other hunters went out on opening day to bring down the first available buck. That was too easy. He would wait until late in the season, when the prey was limited to animals wise enough to have survived the early rush. He liked the challenge for its own sake. He always met it.

In the past couple of years his interests had turned to flying and scuba diving. He'd scored as high on his diving test last month as anyone his instructor had ever seen, and the flying was going well too. My, he loved the feeling of being up there in a plane, and when Norm had told him to take the Cessna off that morning, even though they'd talked about his being the pilot when they'd planned the trip, he'd grinned in pride, as his son Geoffrey did when he was showing off his new bike.

The first leg of the trip, from Estevan down to Williston, was easy. Norm radioed ahead, so the U.S. Air Force would know who they were. Those guys could get pretty snotty, and Norm had told Brent about more than one pilot who'd strayed innocently across the border only to be buzzed down by the military. There was no need to file a flight plan, Norm said. In Canada you were supposed to file when you went more than twenty-five miles from your home base, but small aircraft traffic over the States had got so heavy in recent years, and so many pilots had wanted to call in their plans on the radio, that flight plans weren't mandatory any more. Anyway, they'd just be following the Soo Line most of the way. The sky was heavy, but visibility was fine and the land looked clean and white below.

It had been the worst winter in Saskatchewan since sometime in the thirties, with one stretch of over a month when the temperature never got above zero, and there was still snow covering most of the ground. There'd be floods this spring, for sure. Norm said it would cut into his crop-spraying business. He was hoping for an early start on planting. He'd been counting on a good year this year. He needed it.

Brent had a moment of concern after they landed at Williston. The woman who came out of the airport office to check them over for customs looked pretty severe. This could be trouble. As a convicted felon – that was what he was, although he didn't like to think of it, and especially didn't like talking about it with the family around – he could be stopped at the border, and who knew what they had written down at the checkpoints these days? It sure took a long time to forgive a guy. As a member of AA, he'd had to submit to a psychiatric examination before he could start taking his flying lessons; he sometimes wondered if it would have been easier if he'd still been drinking. Well, at least he could *prove* he was sane, he thought. How many pilots could do that?

The woman at Williston turned out to be friendly enough. She just asked them the routine questions about the purpose of their trip – business and pleasure – and how long they intended to be in the United States. No one mentioned the dog. Time enough to cut that red tape when they reached it.

Norm went in to check the weather forecasts and to buy some maps. Everything looked fine, he said when he returned. Just a straight run across flat country: not much different from Saskatchewan. As Brent lifted the Cessna off the ground – she came up easily with a little less fuel – Norm folded the maps to show the parts they'd be using. Norm gave him the bearings for Livingston, which sat just where the land would start to rise into mountains.

Donna was really chirpy coming out of Williston, pointing down at the red and white stripes of her father's Kentucky Fried Chicken restaurant and noticing every sight along the way: a herd of deer here, a van on the highway there that reminded her of the one her father had just bought for the family. There was little traffic in the air, but they saw an orange plane landing at a small country airport, and Donna remarked on how it stood out against the snow.

"One thing about these small planes," Don said, "you can sure see the country."

Brent winked at Norm, but Norm seemed lost in thought.

At Livingston, where they stopped again for fuel and directions, they all got out of the plane. They were impressed by the facilities at the airport control tower: a comfortable office, with an adjoining room where the weather guys took their coffee, even though Livingston couldn't have been much bigger than Estevan. Aviation people seemed pretty professional down here. Not that Canadians weren't pros. It was just that these people seemed to have a better handle on what they were doing. And friendly! The woman who sold them the gas offered to lend them her car – a white '65 Pontiac, Brent remembered – if they wanted to go into town to get something to eat. But they said they'd better press on to Boise.

They went into the coffee room, where there was candy and stuff laid out on what the guy there called a buddy system – just take what you need and leave the money – but because they had only Canadian change, they grabbed just a couple of cans of pop. There were cigarettes in the fridge, the man said, but Brent didn't bother to pick any up. He did smoke an American brand, and he liked to buy them by the carton, but that could wait till Boise. He had enough to last him. None of the others smoked.

Brent and Donna looked at a couple of maps on the wall.

"Look," Donna said, "there's Yellowstone Park down there. I'd really like to see that."

"It's out of our way," Brent said.

There were some red pins stuck into one of the maps, and Brent asked about them. Something about accidents. He didn't pay much attention.

Norm had spent a long time huddled over the counter in the flight service station, getting as full a briefing as he could on the weather and poring over the relief maps the flight station man had brought out. The weather talk was full of aviation words – "sigmet," "convective," "pirep." It was like a doctor trying to tell you what was wrong with you and impress you at the same time with his vocabulary. But Norm appeared to understand, and the guy doing the briefing was friendly and helpful. The telex machine behind the counter, plugged into a network of computer information from all over the western United States, seemed to spew out as much about the weather as you'd need to know, but Brent remembered the man who was going over the sheets with Norm saying he'd wished he'd had more direct stuff from radar.

One bit of the conversation stuck in Brent's mind.

"These letters here," the weather guy said, "UUA, they mean a pilot has called in about severe turbulence. That's from up around

Burley, in Idaho, and it came on the wire just a few minutes before you got here. UA – that's a computer code – draws our attention to it, but the two U's mean it's urgent, and it goes right out as soon as somebody receives it. There's other turbulence too – that's what the convectives are – but I think we can get you around them."

The flight station man and Norm worked out a route to avoid the worst of the weather. The route was shaped like a sickle, with Livingston at the end of the handle and Boise on the point of the blade. They could fly from Livingston pretty well straight west, to Bozeman, and then Whitehall, and then swing south along the curve of the sickle to Dillon and then into Idaho, actually going well below Boise before they came back up. You could see on the relief maps: the curve would take them through a whole series of mountain passes that followed one another as though a giant river had swept through the mountain ranges eons ago. It might take them a bit longer, the flight station men had said, and even get them to Boise after dark, but it would keep them out of the worst of the weather that was reported ahead. With the Cessna fully loaded – fifty-four gallons in the tanks as they set off – they wouldn't want to try flying over it, and this way they could get past all the mountains at well under their maximum height. By the time they got to Burley, where the UUA was, and which was the last major reference point before Boise, they ought to be well clear of the turbulence; it appeared to be localized.

Don had been on the phone all this time, trying to get through to Jimmy Robertson, the man who was bringing Donna's dog from his home in Weiser, Idaho, down to Boise. When he got him, he called over to Norm to ask how long they'd be getting to Boise. It was nearly four o'clock then.

"About three hours and fifteen minutes," Norm said.

The man behind the weather counter looked as if he was going to say something, but he remained silent. Norm wrote down a list of the VOR reference points on the back of an envelope.

When they got back into the plane, Norm set the radio, folded out his maps, and gave Brent the word to go.

As the plane wobbled and shook into the air of the mountains themselves, Norm took control of the flying. There was no need to discuss the exchange. One moment, Brent was in charge from the co-pilot's seat, feeling only occasional pressure from Norm's feet on the pedals, reinforcing his judgement, or correcting small errors. The next, Norm's hands were guiding the wheel, and the senior pilot was in command.

"Pretty soupy," Norm said.

Soupy? Geez. Well, Norm must have seen worse.

Brent needed his coffee. Not only for himself, but as a gesture. The Cessna was really rocking now and ... well, *he* wasn't scared, but it would be a good sign to Donna and Don. If only the goddamn cup would sit still.

"You'll never get to bring your dog back," Don said to Donna. "He'll bounce all over in his cage and he'll be crazy by the time we get him home. Better just leave him there. We can come down another time and pick him up in a car."

"Daa-ad!"

"Just kidding. You okay?"

"Sure. Okay."

"Feel better now that Norm is flying?"

"Brent was doing all right."

"Just the same ..."

Was Norm still on the path of the sickle? Brent wondered. With the plane bouncing so severely, it was hard to tell. Had he turned south? Couldn't tell. It was hard to concentrate with the stall-horns sounding. Norm had been giving him the headings from the list on his envelope, but Brent had lost track of the turns.

Norm kept peering into the snow that drove into the windshield. His smile grew tighter.

Below them, Donna could make out letters cut into a hillside: CHALLIS VIKINGS. She tapped Brent on the shoulder, and pointed. Brent shrugged.

They were right in the middle of the mountains now. Through the snow they could make out the shapes of the peaks; some were below them now, and on either side, rising ghostlike out of the cold. Norm had the engine leaned right out – the purest mixture of gasoline and oxygen pumping into the Lycoming – and the noise of its struggle droned under the honk of the stall-horns. The Cessna bounced like a wild colt. Donna wanted to lie down on the floor, but there wouldn't be room. She smiled thinly at her father. He looked strained, but he returned the smile. He patted his seatbelt. She nodded.

Norm wasn't playing with the radio now. He had both hands on the wheel, and he was straining to see into the clouds of snow.

Brent looked at the altimeter. Just under 10,000. Some of the crags around them must go as high as –

"Whoops!" Norm said as the plane took a sudden drop.

"Hold her, Norm," Brent said.

"She's going fine."

"Any height left?"

"Doesn't seem to want to go up. We can get through here."

"Where are we?"

"On our way to Boise."

"You going over?"

"Just ... pick ... my ... way ... through these ... oops! That was a bad one." The bumps were coming more frequently now.

"Wish there was some more coffee."

"Wait till she smooths out."

"What'll I do then? Make some in the galley?"

"Get some at – Oh oh."

They needed more power. If only Norm could get her into a dive, she'd pick up enough air speed to lift them over that next ridge. Couldn't be as bad over there.

"I'm going into that canyon," Norm said to no one in particular.

The Cessna twisted into an opening between two mountains, one end of a valley. Norm sought the central line, holding altitude as long as he could, waiting, waiting to go into a dive for more momentum. That was the key: get the Cessna up and then swoop down to regain speed. Ahead, they could see the end of the valley, rising into what – it was now evident – was the steep slope of one of the higher mountains. The valley was a cul-de-sac. He would need every ounce of power the Cessna could muster to climb out the other end.

Worse, they could now see they had entered the valley at its lowest end. The floor below them sloped upward toward the blind exit. The longer he waited to dive the less room there would be below him.

Into the next seconds went all the skills of Norm Pischke's twenty years of flying, all the learned abilities that had become as instinct until the plane had become an extension of his own body. No need to think about how to move the plane in the tortuous air, only to try to ride each new surprise of the whirling currents, to *will* the aircraft over the mountainside that rushed toward the windshield.

Now: *Dive!* Let the engine work with gravity and pull the plane down till there was enough speed to rise again. There! The stall-horns faded as the airspeed grew. Flaps down. Swing her up again ... lift, *lift*, goddamn you. Get over the ...

There was not enough power. She couldn't get over. Too late to turn and run. They were going in.

Norm's big hands moved quickly among the controls. Switch off the magnetos to lower the chance of explosion. Fire could kill them even if they survived the impact that was now inevitable.

Hold the flaps at twenty degrees. Get her in there *soft*.

The Cessna seemed to hang suspended above the sloping canyon wall.

Try to keep the nose up so she'll go down on her belly.

The images through the window seemed to turn to still pictures: the ominous white of the snow, a huddle of black rocks and, jutting straight upward in angular contrast to the slope of the wall, the trunks of dead trees.

Just ease her in there.

"I ... We're going to –" There was no time to finish his sentence.

He just hoped the others were sitting tight.

The trees were bigger than they'd looked.

Here it came. The plane ... was ... He'd lost ... Oh, Jesus!

The impact was not clean. A naked tree trunk ripped into the leading edge of the left wing, spinning the Skyhawk out of its belly-first downward motion. But it was too late to drive the nose straight into the ground. Metal met snow and rock. The tricycle of the undercarriage crumpled. The starboard wing bounced against a boulder. Glass shattered. Waves of shock rippled through the canyon floor, tearing through the guts of the four people strapped into their seats.

Up the hill the plane skidded and bounced ... ten, twenty, forty feet. It shuddered to a sudden stop. The propeller, now turning on momentum alone, drove itself into the snow.

Norm's head was thrown forward and down. His temple hit the extended handle of the throttle. The metal pierced his skull.

From the shattered windshield, a shard of glass jammed against Brent's throat, slicing through the flesh and muscle of his neck. His left shoulder was driven against the dashboard. Bone crunched.

In the rigid back seat, seatbelts held the father and daughter from being hurled toward the windshield. Mercifully, the force of the crash, strong enough to have ruptured spleens or split livers, wiped consciousness from all their minds.

Silence settled. The carcass of the Cessna lay white in the snow. On its dash, the altimeter read 9,750 feet, beside it, the electric clock continued to turn toward the hours of evening and night.

II
The Canyon
May 5 to May 19

Chapter Two

It was weird. Like a dream. Not a nightmare – it wasn't real enough to be a nightmare – but one of those dreams where she knew she was dreaming and wanted it to stop but at the same time was afraid it would. Time seemed to be moving back and forth, and there were no real shapes she could make out, and no real colours; just greys and blacks and different kinds of whites. Mostly whites. Sometimes it seemed as though she was out of her body, or as if she were there and her body were somewhere else, but she didn't even know where *there* was.

As consciousness dawned, so did the hurt. Her legs hurt – worse than anything she could remember. Her whole body hurt. But her legs were the worst. They wouldn't move. Nothing would move. It was as though the pain was holding her down. It was half-light, but still kind of dark. Or maybe the dark was coming in over the light. She couldn't tell. She tried to force her eyes into focus, to *make* herself see. Maybe if she could see something she'd get out of the dream.

That was Brent on the seat in front of her. That was right. Brent had been flying the plane. No, wait a minute … Brent had been flying for a while, but it was Norm's plane they were in, and Norm had taken over. But it had been warm and now she was cold. It was the mountains. She remembered some of it now. They'd been flying over the mountains. That's when the weather had turned bad. The little plane had pitched and bucked, and she'd wanted to stop and get out.

Something was wrong with Brent. Blood was dribbling down his chin. Maybe this was part of the dream. She didn't seem to want to do anything about it. The blood looked as if it were coming right out of his mouth. It was soaking into his shirt and his good jacket.

The dream rolled over her again. She was at home and she had her new dog. Why was the dog crying? Where was her dad? She fought her way back to a half wakefulness. Her dad must be beside her. She turned her head. He was there. Right beside her. He was awake. He seemed to be looking at her. She tried to speak to him, but the words wouldn't come out. How had he let this happen to her? What was wrong? Her dad kept looking at her. She couldn't see any expression on his face, but his eyes were alive. He was kind of ... *loving* her. Maybe everything would be all right. If her dad was there, things would be okay.

Sharon Pischke had had a premonition. It wasn't the first time, either. They just came to her. They were hard to explain, just sort of warnings that something was going wrong. Almost a year ago to the day she'd had one, and that was the day Lorne Dewar, who was married to Sharon's sister and was, like Sharon's own Norm, a pilot, had had his accident. Lorne had been flying for Norm, doing some crop-dusting. And later that day the plane Lorne was flying, a Cessna 172, hit a power line. Lorne was killed instantly. Sharon had been emotionally distraught at the funeral, enough to raise curious glances from some of their friends, but she'd never really told anyone why she'd felt it so deeply.

The other premonition she remembered went much farther back, to the time she and Norm had been courting. She'd wakened with a feeling she found so hard to explain. And then word had come through that Norm had been in an automobile accident. She'd never told Norm about that either.

They were married shortly after Norm earned his pilot's licence. For years he'd flown the bush of northern Manitoba: Thompson, Churchill, up into the barren lands, taking in hunters and fishermen, freight, mail, miners, flying some of the continent's toughest country. What a man he was, with his easy manner and his gentle humour. And what a pilot! Even in the tough and competitive world of bush-flying, Norm Pischke's skills became known and respected. He made a down payment on his own plane.

After Lee, their first child, was born, Norm began resenting the time he had to be away from home, and four years later when Trevor arrived, he switched to what the pilots call "ag flying" – skittering over the prairies, dusting the crops with chemicals. They heard of an air business for sale in Estevan, down near the U.S. border. He bundled up Sharon and the boys and flew down there. The business looked good – lots of crop-dusting, some pipeline patrols, some charter business. A pilot of Norm's skills could easily pick up his instructor's licence and earn some extra money teaching. Flying was burgeoning on the prairies in the mid-seventies. They made an offer on the hangar and the three aircraft and worked out a way to acquire the remainder of the ten-year lease.

The business went okay. Not great, but okay. Norm's reputation grew in the community. People liked him. He got his instructor's licence and took pride and pleasure in sharing his skills. He was a good teacher, although sometimes his students were surprised when, after they'd made an error, he'd simply tell them to watch it next time and to be more careful when they were being tested, rather than making them go through the same exercise again. Sharon had even heard some people were quitting Norm's teaching. Thought he was a little too easy-going. That was their problem.

They had their troubles, sure. Who didn't? Sharon, with a ripe figure and soft eyes, attracted more men than she wanted to, and sometimes Norm was jealous. They separated for a while, and Sharon went down east. But Norm came and got her, and now they were together again. Still struggling financially, but they were together. Things would get better. Even this charter that Brent Dyer had arranged could lead to something more. Don Johnson was supposed to have a lot of money. Getting to know him could help. So she hadn't told Norm about the bad feelings she'd had on Friday night; and on Saturday she'd gone out to see them all off just as she always did.

But now it was Saturday night and there was no phone call. Norm always called. Whenever he was out of town he'd phone just to say he was all right, and to wish her and the kids goodnight.

It was after ten now. Still thinking about her premonition, Sharon picked up the phone to call the airport at Boise.

It was light when Donna woke again. As she drifted in and out of consciousness, a night had passed. It was Sunday morning. Snow still blew in the wind outside, and cold swirls were coming in through the remnants of the windshield and through the two shattered windows on the left side. It was achingly cold. Her legs throbbed. Brent remained slumped and apparently lifeless in the co-pilot's seat. The pilot's seat was empty. Norm was nowhere to be seen.

Donna turned to look at her father, still beside her on the rear seat. His eyes were open, as they'd been when she'd looked at him before, but now his mouth hung slack and his head had fallen back across the back support. He was dead. She screamed.

"Dad is dead! My dad is dead!"

The screams woke her brother-in-law, whose first awareness was of his own injuries. They were extensive – worse even than he could comprehend now. The blood that Donna had seen came from a four-inch gash in his neck. He had lost vast amounts of blood. His shirt and trousers were drenched. On the carpeted floor at his feet was a bloodstain that, in the haze of his semi-conscious state, seemed to him the size and shape of a pizza.

His jaw was smashed. His lower teeth dangled uselessly inside his mouth, and blood trickled down his throat. His left shoulder throbbed; so did his left foot, the one nearest the crimson "pizza" of blood.

He sensed, rather than saw or felt, the snow blowing in around him, and he was certain his life was over. As he came near wakefulness, his semi-conscious mind told him he was about to die, that he should pray, and he formed in his mind a litany, not in the language of any formal religion but in that of the person he'd become. If it was his time to go, well, he'd had fun. He'd sinned a lot – oh Lord, how he'd sinned. He'd stolen and he'd lied – lied to almost everyone, even to himself. Cheated. Done just about anything to serve his own selfish needs. But God knew that, he thought, and he, Brent, knew that if

God wanted to take him, well, that was up to God. He'd just lie there, and let whatever was to happen, happen.

The impact of the crash had torn off Brent's wristwatch. As he struggled back to consciousness he was aware of the dull grey light but had no idea how much time had passed. He might have been asleep for days, he thought. In fact it was only hours. It was Sunday afternoon, and the storm continued. The pilot's seat was empty. He turned his head to look at Donna. There was something about what he saw that was out of place. Something had happened. His bleary mind took several moments to figure out what it was.

Don's jacket – his brown leather sportscoat with the flap pockets and the buttoned shoulder patches – was now draped across Donna's chest. Its collar was tucked under her chin and the sleeves wrapped around her hips, a blanket against the cold. Don was dead – Brent could see that now – but somehow he had managed to pass the jacket over. He must have unfastened his seatbelt, writhed free from the coat and placed it over his injured daughter. Only then had he slumped back to the position he held in death. Before he died, Don had given "the kid" one last present.

Dazed as he was, Brent began to grasp the significance of what he saw. He wanted to share it with his sister-in-law.

"He's dead, Donna," he said, "but he wanted you to live." And then tears welled up in Brent's eyes, and, unable even to reach for each other across the space from the front seat to the back, to hold each other in comfort against their grief and fear, the two wept until exhaustion overcame them again.

Outside the cabin, moving clumsily through the blowing snow, Norm thrashed and rummaged around the outlines of the wreck. His most visible injury was a dreadful one. The steel shaft of the throttle had peeled away the skin from the left side of his skull just ahead of the ear, torn through the temporalis muscle underneath it, and lacerated the bone, exposing the dura that covers the brain, ripping through its delicate fibre, so that part of the yellow-white matter of the brain itself lay bare. On a right-handed person, as Norm was, the part of the brain that was injured is a critical one for expressive speech. An injury to it can, as it apparently had done in Norm's case, leave the victim convinced he can communicate, but unable to do so – "jargon aphasia," doctors call it. What is offered as speech comes out as gibberish, meaningless syllables strung together to form meaningless non-sentences. Connected to the speech centre is the centre of comprehension. Norm could "comprehend" much of what was said to him, but there was no way to tell how much of the rest of his reason he retained. He was moving on and off what medical language calls "islands of rationality."

He returned to the cabin, crawling in through the twisted pilot's door. When Brent woke again, Norm was slouched on the seat beside him, chattering with a fearsome lack of meaning.

Brent's first thought was of warmth. They needed a fire. He had brought with him on the trip a disposable lighter – a yellow, $1.88 Bic. The lighter was still in his shirt pocket.

Somewhere in his rambles outside, most likely in the luggage compartment behind the cabin, Norm had found a can of oil, which he brought, like a puppy with a rubber bone, back to the refuge of the plane. Now, taking the oil carefully from Norm's lap and clutching his lighter, Brent half-rolled, half-fell through the door of his own side. Within crawling distance he saw wood – not vegetation, just a few small sticks jutting through the snow. He gathered enough to make a small pile. Now to open the oil. On the keychain in his trouser pocket was a tiny jackknife, a toy really, less than an inch and a half long, more useful for cleaning fingernails than for practising the art of survival.

He fumbled the knife open and began to jab feebly at the lid of the oil can. He managed to puncture it. He trickled oil over his pile of sticks, and then, using his lighter, ignited a small flame. Trying to keep the weight of his body on his good shoulder, he wriggled across the ground, gathering all the loose sticks he could find and piling them on his fire. Then he stretched out beside it, cradling his head on his arm in a position that he hoped might stop the flow of blood from his neck. In the scant heat of the fire, he fell unconscious again.

From the plane, Donna could see the fire flickering. She could sense its warmth and was determined to get a share of it. She pulled Don's coat over her shoulders like a cape and inched herself across her dead father's legs and out through Brent's door. Not realizing how badly her feet were injured – they were in fact beginning to freeze – she pulled herself erect.

Pain shot through her legs. She fell – forward, toward the fire. Only the reflex action of her arm shielded her eyes from the burning sticks. She rolled over and, using her elbows for locomotion, squirmed around until her feet lay inches from the flame. It was no use. She felt no relief. Before there was any sensation of warmth, one of her socks began to smoulder. Better to be out of the wind.

She crawled back to the plane and, with the help of the still incoherent Norm, clambered into the rear seat, where she fell across the body of her father.

Brent slept on for perhaps an hour. When he awoke, the fire had burned itself out. His body had stiffened in the cold. He called to Donna and to Norm for help. There was no response. He crawled across the snow and clutched at the door. Norm, apparently rational, helped him in as he had helped Donna, and settled him in the co-pilot's seat.

"We've got to have wood," Brent said. "Do you understand that, Norm? Firewood."

Norm attempted to answer. Then, seeming to realize he could not be understood, he held out his hand. Reluctantly, Brent handed him the lighter. Norm, chattering and gesturing, left the plane. They watched him stagger up the hillside that stretched above the plane. In the storm, it was impossible to see beyond that.

Donna looked at her watch. It was three in the afternoon. For the next two hours they waited, trying to comfort each other, although there was no surcease from the pain. They talked of rescue, of how there must be someone in these mountains who could find them. They talked of their families, of how Cindy, who would have expected Brent to have called by now, would be worried, and of Mr. Robertson who would be waiting at the airport in Boise with Donna's puppy, and who would by now have sent up an alarm. Donna's tears stopped. The flow of blood from Brent's throat began to slow. He slipped again into insensibility. Donna hovered in semi-wakefulness. Dimly, she was aware of Norm's presence outside the plane. What was he doing? Her eyes wouldn't focus. He was hunkered down over . . . a log? He was holding the lighter under it. She could make out the flame. There was no smoke. No fire. What was he *doing*? Her consciousness failed again.

Donna woke with a start. At first she had no idea of the time. But it couldn't have been long since she'd fallen asleep; late afternoon light still showed in the broken windows. She realized what had wakened her: Someone was tugging at the coat, her father's leather coat, now pulled tightly around her arms and shoulders. She clutched it back, instinctively holding the smooth leather until, as the pulling continued, she thought her fingernails would be torn away. It was Norm. Half-kneeling on top of her, he was trying to tear away her warmth. She screamed in terror, and for the second time her cries awakened Brent.

"For Christ's sake, Norm," Brent cried. "Get off her! You're hurting her." He tried to pull at the burly pilot from behind.

As if in slow motion, reason began to spread over Norm's face. With a grunt, he slipped to the floor of the plane. For minutes the three stayed silent, panting with exhaustion. And then, like a peace offering, Norm brought forth his prize, an unopened pop-top can of Pepsi-Cola.

Grappling with numbed fingers, Brent got the can open; and huddled in the shelter of the plane's cabin, the three shared the Pepsi in silent communion. It tasted delicious. It was the first nourishment any of them had had in more than twenty-four hours. They drained it.

Suddenly, Norm began gesturing down through the window and pointing down the hill below. He seemed excited, although the words he uttered made no sense. The two young people peered through the snow in the direction he was pointing. Then Brent realized what Norm was trying to show them.

"There are cars down there, Donna," he said. "Can't you see them? Cars. Look, right there, a truck. A welding truck or something. Way down at the bottom of the hill."

"I can't make them out," Donna said.

"I could be wrong," Brent said. "But maybe there's a road down there, and just because of the snow they don't know we're up here. Look. They're really big. Maybe farm machinery."

"I still can't see them. Which way are they going? Are they coming up here?"

"I can't tell. It's like they're not moving at all. Jesus, this snow's thick. But look at that one. That's gotta be a ... I can *see* it. It's a four-by-four. It's yellow. Just like the Sprint that's on the lot back home. We're going to be all right."

As they talked, with their own excitement growing, Norm scrambled once more out the door. Lurching through the snowdrifts, he headed downhill, past the plane's tail assembly, now falling, now stumbling. They could hear his cries over the sound of the wind. His syllables became briefly intelligible.

"Yo-oh," he was hollering, in a shout that Brent remembered as being typical of Norm's greetings when he'd just landed at his own airport. It was a combination of greeting and salute. "Yo-oh."

Still shouting and waving, Norm disappeared behind a bend in the canyon wall. The snow abated, for a moment, and the view down the hill was clearer.

"They're not cars," said Donna. "They're not *anything*."

"I know," said Brent. "I was so sure, too. That four-by-four. I could have sworn I saw that. It's a ... I don't know. It's a rock. They're not moving."

"Maybe Norm will find something."

"Sure," said Brent. "There's gotta be something down there. Someone's got to come."

The mirage of the cars and the disappointment that followed its evaporation had shocked them back to a level of alertness neither of them had felt since the plane had gone down. The crash itself remained a blank, a common effect among victims of sudden and violent accidents, and the evening of the first day, the long, dark first night, and the events of the day leading up to Norm's departure stayed muddy in their memories. The shock of the crash and of Don's death, and the deadening cold had numbed their minds almost as much as their bodies.

With no sun, temperatures had been below freezing on the mountain even during the day, and the fire Brent had built earlier in the afternoon had served little practical purpose. They had been lethargic and unfocused, like animals in brief hibernation, drifting in and out of the lowest levels of consciousness. But now, momentarily exhilarated by the possibility that their ordeal might soon come to an end, they began, for the first time, to set deliberately about making themselves comfortable.

The real work could wait till morning. Now, with the light fading rapidly, they had to prepare themselves for the night. Shelter from the snow became their primary concern. The snow was everywhere in the cabin, blowing down from the top of the hill into which the plane's nose pointed and swirling through the broken windshield. In the back of the cabin, it was beginning to drift, piling up around the shoulders of Don's body and lying thickly on the floor.

They started to remove the red covers from the seats. With the two front seats – chairs almost, with backs that tilted forward – the job was easy, but the material, which they stuffed around the broken glass, failed to make the windshield airtight. The material on the back seat was more difficult to take out. Wincing against their own revulsion, they moved Don's body and slid the covering out from underneath. Still not enough. Donna noticed the carpet, partly soaked in blood and covered by snow. It must be nailed down, she thought. But she bent to pull on it anyway. Miraculously, it gave. She pulled some more. A piece of carpet as big as a baby blanket came up in her hand. Together, they jammed it into the last of the broken windows. Dark and cold, the cabin was now at least a shelter from the snow.

The effort had drained them. Tomorrow they'd do more – if they had to. Maybe help would come by then. Maybe Norm would show up.

Brent huddled in the front seat. Donna crawled into the back and tried to stretch her throbbing legs. There was no room to lie down. They slept.

"I don't want to alarm you, Mrs. Johnson," the polite voice of Jimmy Robertson had said on the phone, "but I wonder if you know the call letters of the plane that Don and Donna were flying down in."

That was Saturday night, and now, on Sunday, Evelyn Johnson, alone in the house that Don had built for his family, was worried. Mr. Robertson – Jimmy, he wanted them all to call him because they'd become so close through letters and phone calls about the dog – had waited a long time before he called. He'd heard from Don around four o'clock, and Don had said they'd be delayed. But by the time he called Evelyn he sounded more worried than he'd wanted to let on. He'd begun to ask questions around the Boise airport, and they'd told him he'd need the call letters. Really, he said, it's nothing to get upset about. They must have set down somewhere. It was snowing in Boise and was probably worse over the mountains. Still, if she could just give him those letters . . . .

She hadn't known them. Why hadn't she asked someone and written them down? She, of all people, a former flying nurse. She'd got that job in the early fifties, shortly after she met Don. She'd wanted to be a stewardess, but stewardess positions were hard to come by, even for an RN, in those still-adventurous days of commercial aviation. The Air Ambulance job had given her the money she needed in the years just before her marriage. For more than two years she'd flown in and out of small prairie towns, helping take the sick or wounded to the major hospitals in Regina and Saskatoon.

Her flying years had given Evelyn a healthy respect for airplanes. The ambulance pilots, almost all of them former air force men, were careful and serious flyers, treating their Cessna 195s – larger than the 172 she knew Don and Donna were in now – or their twin-engined Beechcrafts with the same caution she herself exercised over their human cargo.

She remembered one incident in particular. The air ambulance she'd been assigned to had picked up an elderly heart patient in the northwest of the province and had taken off for Saskatoon into the maw of a threatening snowstorm. The flight had seemed rocky, she recalled, but long before she could become too alarmed, the pilot had brought the plane down on a highway, and the patient had been transferred to a ground ambulance. Better a few hours' delay, the pilot had reasoned, than taking a chance on flying into bad weather – even with a critically ill person on board. And that was nearly thirty years ago. Surely Norm what's-his-name, Brent's teacher, whom everyone seemed to have so much faith in, would act with at least as much caution. And he'd have all those new navigational aids at his command.

She wished she'd been able to remember Norm's last name when Jimmy Robertson had called. She could have checked then. She'd thought about calling Brian, but he and Tara were off delivering chicken to an Alcoholics Anonymous banquet – Brent would have been there if he hadn't been so anxious to fly – and then later they'd gone to a movie. She had called the theatre but she'd got a recorded announcement. "Our first show starts at . . . ." She'd waited.

Finally, at 11:30 Saturday evening she had called Brian at home. She hadn't wanted to raise an alarm. Brian had asked if he and Tara should come over. No, she'd said. She'd be all right. Did she want to come over to their place? No, she'd replied, she'd better wait by the phone. Brian had said he'd call Boise in the morning. Now she wondered if he'd found anything out.

Had Brent made sure to file a flight plan? She'd reminded him specifically of that. She hated to nag, she said, but she knew how important they were.

Chapter Three

He was alive.

The understanding – the *wonder* – snapped into Brent's mind like the spark from an ignition and startled him into wakefulness. He was alive and Donna was alive. They had made it through another night. It was ... Monday. That was right. The crash was Saturday and yesterday was gone and now this was their second morning. Don was dead, and Norm had left them, but there were two of them and it was a new day. He wondered if he should pray again. Why not? Thank you, God, he said. Thank you for letting us make it through the night.

"Donna," he said. "You all right?"

"I'm cold."

"Jesus, I'm cold too. I wonder what the temperature is. How are your feet?"

"They hurt. Are you still bleeding?"

Tentatively, he reached a hand toward his throat. It felt dry. He ran a careful finger down the side of his neck, dreading the wet that had frightened him more than he wanted to admit, frightened him as he'd watched his own blood run down onto the floor. It was dry. The bleeding had stopped.

"It's okay."

"You sound funny."

"It's my teeth. They're all shot to hell. They're kind of hanging loose back in my mouth."

"Do they hurt?"

"Not as much as my foot. It's like I've got a toothache down *there*. It's hard not to think about it."

"Did Norm come back?"

45

"I don't think so."

"I must have been dreaming. I thought he was back. I thought Dad was alive. Dad's dead, isn't he? I don't want to look at him."

"But we're alive. And you've got to remember how much he wanted you to live. He gave you his coat. We've got to get out of here. That's the best thing we could do for him. It's like ... it's like he gave his life for you."

Neither felt like moving.

They watched the snow blowing. In the night, the wind had torn away much of the makeshift window covering, and the snow was again drifting into the cabin.

"Brent."

"Uh-huh?"

"You take the coat."

"Your dad's coat?"

"Yes, you take it. You've got less on than I have. I'm okay on top. I've got my kangaroo jacket and my own leather coat under Dad's."

"I can't."

"Just for a while. We've got to get moving. There must be some stuff in the suitcase."

"You only brought that Bauer bag, didn't you?"

"Yes, but there's stuff in it. There's that long pyjama coat. I could put that on. And socks, and some jeans and ... oh, Brent do you know what else is in there?"

"Sure, one down-filled vest, one snowmobile suit, two pair warm boots, two pair woollen mittens ..."

"Don't laugh. My bathing suit's in there."

They had dressed only for the spring they'd expected in Boise. Brent wore a light pair of tan dress pants, a white shirt with brown spots with a tan pullover vest, all topped off by his brown corduroy jacket. He wore no underwear but peeking out between the cuffs of his slacks and the tops of his fashionable suede shoes, were bright green socks.

In addition to the kangaroo jacket – a loose-fitting garment of wool and velour, zippered up the front and named for the pouches into which she could place her hands – and her tailored leather jacket, Donna wore corduroy jeans, white socks, and a comfortable pair of North Star street shoes.

Brent accepted Don's jacket. Before slipping it on, he carefully loosened the blood-stiffened collar of his shirt. His wound remained closed.

"Let's see what else we've got," he said.

They began their inventory.

First the miscellany: a few maps, crinkled and hardened by the crash and the weather, showing the topography of Idaho and Montana, but with no clues to their own location.

"Remember those letters on the hill?" Donna said. "Challis something?"

"Vikings."

"What would that be?"

"Some kind of town, I guess. I can't find it on any of these maps."

"Weren't there more maps?"

"Norm must have them."

The catalogue continued: a fire extinguisher, the pop bottles they'd emptied during the flight, a copy of the *National Enquirer*, some Kleenex, Norm's wallet and glasses, Brent's flight log – his student's record – and a device he used for navigational reckoning, two packages of paper airsickness bags, lined in plastic. Nothing else worth noting. They moved to the luggage.

Norm, accustomed to living out of the plane, had brought nothing but the clothes he'd worn: slacks, turtleneck and leather coat. Even his shoes, they remembered, had been unlaced, and they wondered if he'd done them up before he left.

Donna's Bauer bag was a light compartmentalized leather carrying case of a style much favoured by athletes and other frequent travellers and named for its manufacturer. It contained the pyjama coat she had mentioned – a woollen, hooded bathrobe – and the socks (five pair, all white) and jeans. As well, there was a shirt with a picture of Mickey Mouse on the chest, which belonged to Brent but which Donna had borrowed some weeks ago and now used as her own. There were also toiletry articles, including a bottle of her favourite Charlie perfume and the electric curling iron she took everywhere she went. And, finally, a file-card-sized booklet of forms Donna was using in one of her Grade Twelve classes, and on which she'd intended to do some work during the stopover at Boise.

Donna was crying.

"What is it?" Brent asked.

"I can't help thinking about the bathing suit. I always forget to bring one. Dad reminded me. He said there'd be a swimming pool at the motel."

"Donna, he's dead. We've got to go on by ourselves. You know what we'll do with that goddamn bathing suit? We'll burn the sucker."

Brent's Bauer bag was next.

He, too, had jeans and socks – although only one pair – and toilet articles: a razor and an aerosol can of shaving soap, a bottle of his favourite after-shave, Christian Dior, and some Bonne Bell after-tan lotion.

But the real treasures were the scraps of food that Cindy had stuck in before they left Saturday morning: half a box of Smarties (a brand of candy-covered chocolates), a granola bar, and a package of shelled sunflower seeds.

And finally among the luggage they found Don's Samsonite suitcase. One white dress shirt; one pair of pyjamas; one pair of swimming trunks; one beach robe; a razor and shaving kit containing a bar of soap, a tube of Crest toothpaste, and a small mirror, broken in the crash. And one wire coat hanger.

There was one last package to open: the plane's first-aid kit. It yielded little: some aspirin, gauze bandages and several large adhesive dressings, surgical soap and a bottle of a commercial preparation called Stop-Bleed.

"I could have used some of that last night," Brent said. "I'm still afraid this thing on my neck is going to start again. But what I might do is just have some of those aspirins. My foot hurts stony-ass bad."

"Here, put it under my jacket. Try to warm it against my tummy."

Awkwardly, Brent scrunched into his chair. The pain was rolling over him now, and the effort of trying to be cocky had left him drained. Donna cradled his foot against her skin, but she had little warmth to share.

Brent wanted to cry out, to scream. He could taste something sour in his throat – it reminded him of his drinking days, when he'd vomited until his stomach was empty. He tried to cough it up but all that came out was more of the sour taste. Donna looked terrible. One of her eyes was starting to close, and there were black rings around both of them, like shiners. She was trying to scoop snow from the cabin floor and rub it on his foot. He wanted to pass out from the pain, but he couldn't leave Donna alone.

Then he saw the cut on her hand – an ugly gash that laid open most of her right palm.

"Did you know you had that?" he said.

"I ... I guess so. But I can't feel it. I suppose, like, the rest of me hurts so bad I haven't got room for any more. I just hurt all over."

With the Stop-Bleed, Brent cleaned the wound in Donna's hand, then dressed it with some of the gauze and, with his own hands stiff and clumsy, applied one of the adhesive bandages to her palm. Then they wrapped one of her extra socks around it.

"We've got to get some kind of fire going in here," Brent said. "We could die from the cold. Do you know what Norm did with my lighter?"

"I think I saw him trying to set fire to one of those logs he dragged in yesterday. I was half asleep, but I sort of saw him outside the plane. I couldn't figure out what he was doing."

They found the lighter under the pilot's seat. It was empty of fuel. Sparks shot impotently from its flint.

"Oh, Jesus," Brent said.

"That's what he must have been doing when I saw him," Donna said. "Tried to start a fire and just held it there till it went out. You know how crazy he seemed."

"Listen, I've got an idea. Hand me one of those Coke bottles and the coat hanger from Don's suitcase."

"What are you going to do?"

"There's something a guy showed me just a couple of days ago. Thursday, when I was out at Norm's. There's a little thing under the wing. It drains fuel from the bottom of the tanks. You're supposed to use it to see if there's water in your fuel. The water goes to the bottom, see, and if you open this little valve, you can see if you've got water or gas."

Brent moved to the pilot's seat, next to the right-hand window, so he could use his good arm to push through the makeshift covering.

He straightened out the coat hanger. For several minutes he poked at the valve under the wing, just barely within his reach. Liquid began to drip. Exchanging the coat hanger for the Coke bottle, he reached out again. The drip was just at the farthest reach of his arm. He caught one, two, three drops, and then the flow stopped. He jabbed again with the coat hanger. Reached out again to catch. Jabbed again. Suddenly the liquid began to run freely. He caught almost half a bottle before it stopped. He brought it in and smelled it. It was gasoline.

As quickly as they could move around the cramped cabin, they made a pile of expendable materials on the cabin floor. The Kleenex, the useless maps, the lining of Don's suitcase.

"We'd better save some," Brent said.

He poured gas over the pile and held the lighter at its base. Sparks flew off the flint. He thought momentarily of the remaining fuel in the wing tanks. The hell with it, he muttered to himself. It would be several feet away from any open flame.

The sparks weren't catching. He tried again. Nothing. It wasn't going to work.

Brent thought of a scene from his drinking days, when Jimmy would limit him to five gallons of gas at a time for his car. With his friends, he found a way to supplement his supply. At night, the trucks from the oil fields were parked downtown – always, he discovered, with their tanks full of gas for the next day's work. Brent and his friends used to sneak up the lane where they were parked and siphon off enough fuel for their evening's driving adventures. To simplify the mechanics of siphoning, they used green plastic garbage pails, holding them lower than the trucks' fuel tanks and then raising them above the level of Brent's car. One night, he remembered, he wasn't sure if they'd got enough, and he'd tried to use his lighter to peer into the receiving pail. Va-voomph! The explosion had almost blown his hair off.

"This has got to work," he said now, and bent again to the task. More gas from the bottle. More sparks. Then: fire. Their little pile was burning.

As Brent nursed the flames, Donna began repairing the coverings on the windows, trying to maximize every precious flicker of warmth. It was working. They could feel the heat. In celebration, they opened the sunflower seeds, savouring each one they ate, promising they'd ration every particle of their food. After a dozen of the seeds were gone, they closed the package again. They'd need the rest later. They were going to make it. They'd stay alive.

After the paper, Donna's swimsuit burned best of all.

"You know," said Brent, "when we get out of here I'm going to do a commercial for Bic lighters."

The relief of the fire was short-lived. They had to keep shifting their positions, trying to bring different parts of their bodies near the meagre blaze, and every move was painful. There was no comfortable way they could sit; each position seemed to uncover a new bruise, or to remind them, as with Brent's shoulder or Donna's hand, how serious the injuries they had already discovered really were.

Donna had removed her shoes to rub her feet, and twice, as she tried to toast her toes, Brent had to point out to her that her socks were smouldering – just as they had on the first day, near the ill-fated fire outside. She had no feeling below her ankles.

From the yield of the suitcases, they began to fashion costumes. Donna had slipped the Mickey Mouse shirt over her kangaroo jacket. Over both she still wore her own leather jacket. Now, she slipped into her pyjama coat, pulling up its hood. The fit was snug, but comfortable, and she discovered to her pleasure that the coat was long enough to wrap around her legs. Brent's legs, scrawny to begin with and covered only by his tan slacks, needed immediate insulation. Over the slacks he pulled the bottom half of Don's pyjamas and then, finding little relief, inverted the tops too, and stuck his legs through the sleeves. With Don's leather jacket now worn over his own sports-coat, vest, and shirt, his torso seemed warm enough. As an equivalent to Donna's hood, he fashioned a kind of parka-top from Don's white dress shirt, carefully pushing the extra cloth down inside his own shirt with the coat hanger. The congealed blood on his neck stayed dry. As Donna had, he slipped one of the pairs of white socks over his hands. There was still no sunlight and the snow continued to course around the crash site, but the piercing edge of the freezing night was dulled in the afternoon. For the time being at least, and in the relative warmth of the daytime, they were protected from the cold.

A strange mood came over them. It was almost forty hours – the first night, the first long, fuzzy day, the second night, the bitterness and pain of the second morning – since the crash. Only now could they begin to realize the horror of their situation. The events since the crash – Don's death, Norm's apparent insanity, the injuries that seemed to grow in both number and severity with each exploration of their bodies – all these had passed as a dream. For much of the time their dazed condition had softened the blows of reality. This morning, the tasks of inventory and housekeeping, of starting the fire and assembling their makeshift winter garb, had kept them too busy to reflect. Now, as they rested and tried to find a way to huddle together near the remains of their fire, they knew all too clearly what had happened to them. It was they, Brent Dyer and Donna Johnson, two young people from Estevan, Saskatchewan, and not two strangers they might read about or see on the drive-in screen, who were facing a lonely and savage death on the side of a mountain whose name they did not know. The parents who had seen them through all their troubles before were not there. Don Johnson's lifeless body was reminder enough of that. And yet, somehow, they felt relief. They were alive. The worst should ... *must* be over. They felt almost euphoric. They would survive.

Donna announced that she was going to walk for help.

"You can't do it," Brent said. "You don't even know where we are."

"We've got to be *some*where. There's got to be someone around. Maybe Norm found help. Maybe just because he can't talk he can't tell them where we are."

"We've got to wait here. Norm must have sent some kind of Mayday out before we hit. They've got to be looking for us."

"Do you think he really sent a message?"

"I don't know. I can't remember much of what happened."

"I can't remember anything."

"I've heard people who are in car crashes have the same thing."

"We were flying and then we crashed."

"We'll probably remember it later. We'll probably remember everything. It will all come back to us at once. Don't be scared, Donna."

"I am scared. I'm scared and I'm going to walk for help."

"You're nuts. We should stay here. You can't walk anyway. You can't even stand."

"I'm going."

"I don't even want to talk about it, Donna."

"You still sound funny. Do your teeth hurt?"

"You're fucking right they hurt. I think my jaw's broken. I can feel the bone in there."

"I'm going."

"Oh, for Christ's sake go then."

"I'll bring help."

"You'd be better off here."

"I'll be back. You'll see."

She couldn't pull her shoes on over her swollen feet, so she slipped two of the Cessna's airsickness bags over her socks. She wrapped the hood of her pyjama coat tightly around her neck and put an extra pair of socks over her hands. She opened the cabin door and slithered out through the opening. Tentatively, she put one foot on the ground. She felt nothing. Holding the edge of the door with her elbow to protect the wound in her hand, she started to step onto the other foot, like a swimmer entering an icy pool. She put her weight on both feet. With a cry, she pitched face forward into the snow.

"I can't do it. I can't walk."

"Can you make it back in here?"

"I think so. Can you give me a hand?"

"Just roll over on your back and kind of hinch yourself back up to the doorway. I'll drag you in."

"I'm sorry."

"It's okay. Someone will come."

"Oh, Brent, I'm so scared."

"There's nothing wrong with that. I'm scared too."

"I wish Dad was alive."

"We've got to cover him up."

"You mean, like, bury him?"

"Just cover up his face, I guess. And maybe say some kind of prayer. Like a funeral service."

"You're not supposed to think it's him there any more."

"It isn't."

"I know that but ... he was so *alive*."

"It's not him, Donna. The real him has gone to heaven. That's just his body."

"Do you believe in heaven?"

"In God, sure. In heaven? Yeah, I guess so."

"In church they talk about heaven. Dad never went to church."

"That doesn't mean he couldn't go to heaven."

"The church says it does. I wonder if Mom ever tried to get him to join the church. I'll bet he wouldn't have."

"He wouldn't have done anything he didn't believe in."

"He could go to heaven, though."

"He's not there, is he? Not in that body?"

"No."

There were no extra pieces of clothing to cover Don's face. He lay – sat – where he had died, on the left side of the double back seat. His body had stiffened in death and his feet extended toward the centre of the cabin floor, just behind the front seats, where their fire still flickered. His head lay back on the head rest. His eyes stared upward at the cabin roof. His mouth was open. Together, they raised the upper part of his heavy body and slipped off the beige sweater vest he'd worn over his brown shirt. Brent reached up and pulled the dead eyelids down. They covered the face with the woollen vest.

"Our Father," Brent began, and Donna joined in. She fought back the tears. "Hallowed be Thy name. Thy kingdom come."

They finished the prayer together.

"Do you know any hymns?" Donna said.

"All I can think of is 'Holy, Holy, Holy.'"

Donna started, her young girl's voice clear in the ancient melody, and Brent sang with her.

"Holy, Holy, Holy,
Lord God Almighty.
Early in the morning
Our song shall rise to Thee."

When they finished they sang it again, and then Donna wept, and Brent tried to hold her, and they talked about Don for a while, and then Donna crossed herself and the service was over.

Once again they felt, not the near-euphoria that had come over them as they'd sat earlier by the fire, but still a kind of comfort. Neither spoke for a while, but each was thinking about the strength they had found in the ritual of the Lord's prayer and in the only hymn they had been able to remember. It was something familiar to them, of course, but it was more than that. In the dull, hurting cold interior of the tiny plane, the words possessed – more than ever before for either of them – literal meaning. "Deliver us from evil," they had prayed. They had repeated the same litany thousands of times in church and Sunday school and in the public school system of Estevan; but for the first time the words *meant* something. Deliver *us*, Brent and Donna, from *this* evil, *this* horror, this ordeal. "Give us this day our daily bread." How easy that had been to repeat with the teacher or with the priest, but now it was a plea. In the place they now found themselves the "daily bread" that had always been on their tables would be the rest of the sunflower seeds, the still untouched half-pack of Smarties, perhaps even the toothpaste – *anything*. They were hungrier than they had ever been in their lives.

And thirsty. Their thirst was overwhelming. The last liquid either had consumed was the Pepsi they had shared with Norm almost twenty-four hours ago. Their need for drink was now stronger even than their need for food. Extremes of temperature, the psychological and physical trauma of shock, the altitude at which they had now been for nearly two days ... even the fear ... all these increase the human body's need for nourishment; but just as the body can live longer without solid food than it can without liquid, so does thirst seem a stronger urge to the deprived than actual hunger.

The snow that surrounded them was no solution. Brent was afraid of it. He believed – correctly – that eating snow can be dangerous. It can freeze the mouth; there is so little moisture when it melts that it can serve only to increase the thirst. They had not been able to work out a system to melt the snow. They decided to drink their urine.

"What we'll do," Brent said, "is I'll pee in the Thermos. I think I've got enough in me to get a good drink. It'll at least quench our thirst. Can you get it down?"

"I'll try."

This was the first time either had wanted to urinate since the crash, and Brent was embarrassed about relieving himself in Donna's presence. He turned his back and, fumbling through the layers of his clothing, prepared to put something in the Thermos bottle. Nothing would come.

"It's like giving a goddamn sample," he said. Then, the urine began to flow – dark and brackish in colour. He said nothing. He finished, did himself up again. "Now," he said, "I'll pour some into the top." It looked even worse in the drinking cup, almost red.

"It's got blood in it," he said. "I must have hurt myself inside. Do you want to try to drink it?"

Donna reached out her hand for the cup. Averting her eyes and trying not to inhale, she raised it to her lips and poured a sip into her mouth. Immediately she retched.

"You've got to get it into your stomach," Brent said.

She tried again, retched again. It would not go down.

Brent took the cup from her. His thirst was powerful. He tried to think of coffee, tried to hypnotize himself. It would be wet and would satisfy his need. There was *salt* in it. Surely he could do this, and then maybe if he drank it, Donna could do so too.

He sipped. He could not swallow. It was still warm and bitter and he was sure he could taste the blood. He spat it out. His stomach heaved and bile rose in his throat.

He dashed the cup of red-stained urine out the cabin door.

"I'd die before I could drink that," Donna said.

"I never liked tomato juice in my beer anyway," Brent said.

Donna wept.

Chapter Four

It's really just a question of time until some lummox becomes the focus of a several hundred thousand dollar search effort and afterward admits that his unmodified – yet quite modifiable – ELT is sitting on a shelf in his basement.

— *Canadian Aviation*, September, 1979

On July 29, 1977, Bill Cowan, a Canadian Pacific Airlines jet pilot who, with a couple of his colleagues, flew old-fashioned biplanes in displays of aerobatics for a hobby, was warming up his Pitts Special over Kelowna, British Columbia, when he heard a loud explosion that seemed to come from just behind his head in the open cockpit. Since Cowan had his Pitts in a roll at the time and had other things on his mind, he thought little of the noise. As he came out of the roll, however, he discovered white smoke billowing about his head, and he was very aware of an odour that reminded him of rotten eggs. Although the plane was still flying easily, he took it down to have a look.

He was stunned by what he discovered. The explosion had come from the compartment that carried his ELT – emergency locator transmitter – a device that all Canadian pilots had carried in their aircraft by law since the issuing of a federal regulation in 1974. "No person," said the regulation, "shall operate an aircraft in Canada or a Canadian aircraft outside Canada unless it is equipped with one or more serviceable emergency locator transmitters." Since then, the ELTs had figured in a number of search and rescue operations and had almost cèrtainly saved lives. Small radio devices, about the size of a walkie-talkie, with switches that can be set either to be turned on manually or triggered by impact, ELTs transmit a signal at 121.5 megahertz, a frequency other aircraft keep constantly open. Although the signal travels only along lines of sight, it can be heard for miles and has been received by commercial aircraft flying thousands of feet over the vicinity of a crash their pilots may not even have heard about. The signal serves as a homing device.

The problem lies with the batteries. When the Canadian regulation was issued, virtually all ELTs were powered by lithium, the lightest metal known to man and one whose power capabilities can withstand long exposure to severe temperatures. Over the years of its use, however, more and more examples of its temperamental instability were reported. Cowan's experience was far from unique, and some airports expressed reluctance to allow aircraft carrying lithium-powered ELTs to park in their hangars overnight.

The authorities were now faced with a dilemma: was it more dangerous to carry an instrument that might explode at any time in an innocent aircraft, or to allow planes to fly carrying no emergency locator transmitters at all?

The route the bureaucrats chose was a complex one. First, they issued an order, dated September 1977, ordering all ELTs powered by lithium batteries removed from all Canadian registered aircraft. Then they issued a waiver of the original order, which *allowed* people who had purchased lithium ELTs to have them modified (meaning to have their power systems changed from lithium to a more stable element) and return them to their aircraft, but didn't *order* them to. The waiver was extended. The reasoning, presumably, was that having ordered all owners of aircraft to spend substantial amounts of money to equip themselves, the authorities were reluctant to order them to spend more.

Norm Pischke was one of the pilots caught in this morass of regulations. He had complied with the order of 1974, had purchased, at $275 each, lithium-powered ELTs for all the airplanes he owned. In 1977, following the second proclamation, he had dutifully removed them. Unobligated, and pressed for money, he had not bothered to change the power systems for his safety devices. And when GYVP took off from Estevan in May of 1979, it was, quite legally, without an emergency locating device. The orange, lithium-powered NARCO 10 ELT Norm had purchased for his Skyhawk rested on a work-bench in his hangar.

None of these technical details, of course, mattered to the two young people on the mountainside. All they knew was that there was no ELT where Brent thought there might be one – in the luggage compartment. Its mount was there, a metal frame that appeared to have been set in to hold the ELT, but it was maddeningly empty.

Equally maddening was their inability to get a sound, even the hiss of white noise, from the radios. The radios were dead. No amount of fiddling with the knobs could produce a single crackle, although beside them on the dashboard the electric clock continued to display the correct time.

"It takes hardly any power to run the clock," Brent explained. "If Norm turned the switches off the crash must have knocked them back on again. Anyway, the batteries are dead. The radios won't work." Even so, once, when Brent was asleep, Donna tried playing with them. In desperation, she whacked the radio as hard as she could with her good hand – and was disappointed when there was no result except a shock of pain. It *should* have worked.

The days from Monday to Friday, from the second full day of their ordeal until the sixth, were excruciatingly similar, full of pain and thirst and hunger and despair, but marked by constant and recurring waves not only of hope but of joy – joy in their survival and, increasingly as the days droned by, in what they were learning about their own capacities to cope and to persevere and, more than anything, to live.

They talked often of love, and the talk was naked and without shame. In the same way that physical necessity was stripping away their modesty about their bodies, the circumstances of their lives – bounded as they were by their inability to move from the cabin of the plane – were eroding the reticence they'd felt from childhood about their own emotions. They wept openly with one another, and sometimes it seemed to them as if the weeping had been orchestrated, so that when one broke down the other found some extra reserve of determination to compensate. Brent would begin talking about his children, about how much they meant to him and what he would do for them when he saw them again, and then the reality of the odds against that ever happening would sweep over him, and Donna would react with anger. "You're not going to let those kids down," she would say. "You've got to get back to them. You're not leaving *my* sister alone."

Cindy. They talked a lot about Cindy – both of them, but mostly Brent. She'd been fourteen when Brent first saw her, three years younger than Donna was now. She'd been serving chicken in Don's restaurant. He'd gone in to buy a bucket and some french fries to take back to the place where he and his cronies had been drinking beer. He was immediately struck by her, for even then she showed the signs of the woman she would become, slim and blonde, with the Johnson blue eyes. He'd even asked for a date – he'd been a little drunk, to tell the truth – but she'd refused. She knew about Brent Dyer; who in town didn't? Besides, even if she'd wanted to go out with him she knew what her parents would think. They'd known him almost as long as they'd been in Estevan. Their acquaintance began, in fact, shortly after Don had first opened a restaurant and, to supplement the family income, had opened a driving range behind it, where players could bang golf balls out into the valley beyond. There were a surprising number of grass fires in the valley and often after one of the fires one of the local ragamuffins would show up with a bag of used balls to sell to them. The ragamuffin was Brent. They knew, of course, that he'd been picking the balls out of the burned-over area, and they shortly put an end to the transactions. What they didn't know – as Brent now told Donna – was who had set the grass fires in the first place. Brent 'had. He was eight at the time, and trying to learn to smoke cigarettes.

The teenage Brent had persisted in his courtship of the cool and beautiful young blonde. He was, for all his wild reputation, not an unappealing person. Even then he had an undeniable charm, a kind of indomitable cheekiness. He was quick of wit and as quick to laugh at other people's smart remarks as at his own. He could, when he wanted to, cloak his arrogance with what appeared to be a boyish shyness. Certainly he was something of a braggart, but often his boasting seemed to spring more from sheer delight in his own accomplishments – even his illicit ones – than from an attempt to impress his listener. He didn't look like much, heaven knows, with the long hair he was so proud of. And at five foot seven he was scarcely taller than Cindy. But there was something about him.

Besides which, he had wheels. Jimmy always saw to that. He laughed when he told Donna. Cindy agreed to meet him for a movie.

Before long they were keeping steady company, although Cindy sometimes had to be less than frank with her parents not only about whom she was going with, but about where she was going.

There is not much to do in Estevan. The Dairy Queen, or DQ, as the young people call it, provides a convenient meeting place. But the theatre on the main street changes movies infrequently. There are dances almost every week, but mostly the kids, as they say, make their own fun. The best place to make that fun is the drive-in theatre. Brent and Cindy began going to the drive-in. They also began going away on weekends when they could think of convincing stories for Cindy's parents – not frequently, but whenever they could manage. Not long after her fifteenth birthday, Cindy became pregnant.

It was not a forced marriage, not in the shotgun sense anyway. Even as he talked to Donna about it, Brent laughed at how people had used that phrase. If anyone had forced the marriage, in fact, it had been Brent and Cindy themselves. Abortion was never discussed, and not only because of Cindy's Catholicism. The baby was real to her as soon as she knew she was pregnant. When Don and Evelyn had said in their quiet way that if Cindy, er, didn't want the child they could raise it as their own, she had quickly demurred. It was her baby – hers and Brent's – and she was going to look after it. They wanted the child as much as they wanted each other. They could make things work out. They were convinced they were in love, and the more the families opposed their marriage, especially the more the Johnsons would talk about Brent's reputation and his drinking, the more stubborn they became. They *wanted* each other.

They tried to run away. Brent broke into his father's garage for what he swore was one last time and left a note. "I just told him I loved him," Brent said to Donna, "and I promised him I'd never do anything like that again." And then he borrowed a car from the lot. The next morning, full of remorse, they called home, and both families told them to come back and get married properly. The service could have been held in the Catholic church, but because of their age the priest had wanted them to take a course in marriage first, lasting several weeks, and they hadn't wanted to wait that long. The Dyers arranged for a ceremony at their own St. Paul's United.

Don drove Cindy to the church; on the way there he'd told her one last time that if she wanted to back out he'd stand by her. But Cindy had said no, this was what she wanted.

Donna was ten the year they got married, too young for bridesmaid, as Cindy said, and too old for flower girl. She remembered the ceremony, though. It was the first time she'd been in a Protestant church. Cindy had looked lovely, and Donna could still see her walking down the aisle, clinging to their father. That was funny, she thought: it was one of the few times she could remember any really close physical contact between her father and Cindy. Cindy had really been holding on.

For a wedding present, Jimmy Dyer had given the young couple the bungalow on Nicholson Road, worth $28,000 at the time, in the same prosperous part of the town where both sets of parents lived. Brent had been eighteen, three years older than his pregnant bride, and no one in Estevan had thought the marriage would last.

"But *I* did," Brent said now. "And the funny thing is I'm more in love with her now than I was then."

"But you guys fight all the time."

"We love each other," Brent said. "That's more important than fighting."

"How do you know when you're in love?"

"Come on, Donna."

"How do you know?"

"You just know. Are you in love with Ron?"

"I think so. There's never been anyone else, anyway. Yes. Yes, I am."

"Well, how do *you* know?"

"Because he wears white socks?"

She giggled. And then Brent giggled. And then both of them giggled together. For a while, they were back at home.

Day by day through this period – from Monday, the second day of their isolation, until Friday, the sixth – the landscape outside the

62

plane, which had at first appeared to them as only an undefined series of white shapes, took on more of a reality. The hillside into which the Cessna had crashed was not a steep one. At the point of impact it ran upwards at about forty-five degrees, but above the nose of the plane it took a sharp upward swoop, so that looking through the space where the front windshield had been they could see no sky. The slope was covered by thick snow, but it was dotted with windblown evergreens – "Christmas trees," Brent called them; and here and there a hardwood, stripped bare by winter and wind, stood erect and brown. The largest of these dead trees was the one the plane had hit; it stood behind and slightly below them now. Beyond it the hill continued to drop, like the bed of some huge and barren river whose banks were the mountains that rose on either side. Most forbidding was the peak off the plane's left wing. It loomed toward the sky, its summit invisible in the gushing snow, and it shielded them from the sun for much of each day.

Peering downhill they could see clearly that what they'd mistaken for cars or trucks in their first hours of consciousness were in fact rocks, boulders really, although from the distance it was hard to get a true sense of their size. Beyond the rocks, the downward angle of the valley turned to the left, and if there was lower land beyond, it was hidden by the slope of yet another mountain. They were, clearly, at one end of a canyon, perhaps a mile in length and maybe much longer, and even when there was some sun it hung over their heads for only a few hours a day.

The talk on the mountain turned frequently to mundane matters. In exquisite detail one day, Brent described what he would do for the patio of the house on Nicholson Road. Last fall, with good intentions, he had bought green indoor-outdoor carpeting to cover the patio, to turn it into a kind of extension of the house, but he'd never got around to laying it. Now he told Donna how he'd cut each yard of the material until it fit the patio as tightly as paint, and how he and Cindy would have barbecues there and listen to the children laugh. In her turn, Donna talked of her plans to finish the school year, and to graduate with her class, and then maybe to think about settling down with Ron. Maybe Ron could get work at Dyer Ford. He was good with body work – *auto* body work, she said when Brent laughed. There was one long discussion about whether Evelyn, Donna's mother and – they found themselves able to say this now – Don's widow, ought to join Brent's bowling team.

And they talked of God. At first it was hard to do that, but when they began to open up about how each of them had felt during their funeral service for Don, they were able to discuss their feelings about divinity without embarrassment. Brent explained the ideas of Alcoholics Anonymous – that he, like the other people he'd met there, had been able to overcome his need to drink only by the help of what AA called a "higher power." In AA, the name of that higher power was incidental to one's acceptance of its importance. On the mountain, though, the power was becoming real to him. It was God, the Lord. More and more – and with less and less self-consciousness – he found himself talking to Donna about "the Lord." "The Lord wants us to survive," he would say. "The Lord stopped the bleeding from my neck." Or, "We should thank the Lord the plane didn't catch fire."

When at last on Wednesday they woke to clear weather, they knelt in a prayer of gratitude. It had been five days since the crash, and snow had fallen on every one. It was the Lord who had given them this sign that He would bring them through.

These were not easy ideas for them to accept. Donna had been brought up, at her mother's insistence, in the Catholic Church, and would have described herself as Catholic and a believer. But the Church had been remote from her, and abstract; belief in God no more important to her than her belief in the abilities of her baton teacher. And Brent, as much as he acknowledged the power that had helped him conquer his drinking problem, was at his core a doubter of anything so formal as an Almighty with a true presence. Yet on the mountain, the idea, the *force*, to which they gave the name of God became real to them. He was there. There was no specific point at which the realization came over them, but gradually they moved from seeing themselves as two people alone to talking as if there were three of them on the mountain: Donna and Brent and the Lord.

Donna's appearance deteriorated steadily. The smoke from their meagre fire had already settled into her once shiny hair so that it hung in a smelly scraggle over her forehead. Her right eye was swollen almost shut, and discoloration flooded not only the flesh around it but the eye itself; a blood vessel appeared to be broken so that her blue iris resembled a bull's eye in a field of red. The Stop-Bleed had helped to soothe the palm of her hand, but there was still severe pain.

The pain was worst during the nights. They were never able to find comfortable positions to sleep in. They kept the backs of the two front seats bent permanently forward, to afford the largest possible area of flat space, but they were still unable to find a combination of sitting, kneeling, or lying down in which either of them could stay comfortably. Each new position revealed new variations of pain. "If I haven't got my head in a snowbank I've got a pedal up my ass," Brent said. But it hurt to move too, so they would stay as still as they could for as long as they could, hoping to drift off, and move only when the pain became intolerable. Unable to share each other's body heat, they concentrated on preserving as much as possible of their own. Brent would tie his own feet inside one of the elastic-trimmed seat-covers they'd removed and then, bending into a sit-up position, would help Donna tie hers. Try not to toss and turn, he would tell Donna. Each night they said the Lord's prayer.

Dreams would race with stunning clarity through their fitful sleep. Sometimes these dreams would take them far from reality, and there was one night when Brent was so certain he was once again on a weekend trip to British Columbia with Cindy that he began talking aloud, and with such compulsive happiness that he wakened Donna and frightened her with his inability to comprehend where they really were.

"I thought you were crazy," Donna said.

"It was sure nice there," Brent replied.

But perhaps the most touching of their dreams, and the most frustrating, were fantasies based on the crash. They dreamed of jet planes with giant magnets, and of people coming to take photographs. On the night after he'd dreamed of Cindy, Brent imagined himself rising from the hillside and travelling to a nearby town ("I think it was that place where we saw the sign about the Vikings," he told Donna when his mind was clear again) and bringing back requirements for their most immediate needs: bandages for Donna, some more aspirins for his own aches and several bottles of Coke.

"I can't understand it," he told Donna. "I was out of here and I got the stuff, and I got my change and everything, and then I brought it back here. I didn't even tell anyone where we were."

Chapter Five

At half past noon on Monday, Glen Raney placed a long distance call to the office of the search master at Boise. "I think we may have something here," he said.

By coincidence, Raney was the last person to have seen the people aboard GYVP. In aviation jargon he was LVM FSS, in charge of the Livingston, Montana, Flight Service Station, and it was to his office that Norm Pischke had gone for advice on the best route for the last leg of their journey. That was Saturday afternoon, forty-four hours ago, and, along with most of the other members of the Montana and Idaho aviation community, Raney was becoming increasingly certain that the plane had gone down; if they'd taken emergency shelter, someone would have heard by now.

Raney remembered Norm as friendly and, as they had pored over the maps and weather bulletins, attentive. An easy brief, he had called it, although he had wondered if Norm appreciated the ferocity of the terrain he was about to enter. He had also wondered about a flight plan; Canadian pilots were used to filing flight plans. He remembered Brent, too. The young man had been talking with the girl, but he'd stopped to look at the relief map of the country between Livingston and Boise and had asked about the dozen or so red pins stuck into it. "Those are what we call fatals," Raney had told him. "That's just the last few years." It hadn't seemed to impress the young man.

Raney remembered the time of their arrival without even having to look at his log. Jo Ann Ferguson had been a little slow coming out of the Yellowstone Air Service office to gas up the plane, and when she'd finally got to the pumps she'd said she was sorry but she'd wanted to watch the end of the Kentucky Derby, so it must have been just before four o'clock. Jo Ann had offered to lend them the Ferguson's old Pontiac to go into town and get something to eat. "That's nice of you," the pilot had said, and Jo Ann had gone round to get the car, but the third man, the oldest one, who'd asked to use the phone and had used his credit card for long distance, had thanked her and said the snack food they could get at the airport would be enough; they'd better get going. They'd climbed into the plane and sat on the runway for several minutes. They'd left at 4:01. That was on the log.

Now Raney – LVM FSS – was acting in another capacity. He'd had a call from a man he knew vaguely, a local pilot named Les Hudson. Hudson had been out ploughing his garden on Saturday afternoon and he'd seen a Cessna – white with what looked to him like dark blue trim – heading toward Paradise Valley to the south. A 172? Hudson wasn't sure, but it had the right swept-tail design. No, he hadn't seen the call letters – or hadn't remembered them if he had. Altitude? About 7,500, Hudson had figured, and he'd remembered thinking the pilot must have been crazy. You could *see* the front coming at him, and the weather had looked – Raney had a note of his word – "crummy." The plane would be in the thick of it about twenty minutes after Hudson had made his sighting, right over Rock Creek. He'd thought they were on their way to Yellowstone.

In Boise, Worthie Rauscher wrote down the details of Raney's report in a bold hand and felt a flicker of hope. The information was passing down the line. This was the first clue of the search.

Tracing a missing aircraft is a combination of science and hunch, but it is as methodical as painting a house. And nowhere in the world is the method more refined and sophisticated than it is in the northwestern quadrant of the United States, for the very obvious reason that a lot of planes go down there.

The mechanics of the search had gone into unofficial motion on Saturday night, following Sharon Pischke's anxious telephone call and Jimmy Robertson's persistent questions in Boise. As of 9:25 Sunday, the search was officially "on," so declared by the officers of Scott Air Force Base on the Missouri-Illinois border. The base was more than a thousand miles from the plane's last sighting, but, with its banks of computers and trappings of command, it was empowered to formalize the procedure. Boise, as the presumed destination of GYVP, became the centre of planning; Worthie Rauscher, as administrator of the aeronautics division of Idaho's department of community affairs, became search master. The acronymic language of aviation spelled out Rauscher's first moves: an INREQ – an information request to all stations along the possible route of the missing plane, to see if any of them had heard of its whereabouts; and an ALNOT – an alert notice that places the entire aeronautical system on watch.

Did the Cessna have an ELT? A quick check with Sharon Pischke gave them the bad news. Unless the plane were broadcasting from its radio set – unlikely as the INREQ brought in negative responses – the search would be primarily visual.

The technical resources at Rauscher's command were formidable. Even in the wilderness of the high cordillera, radar scans the sky continuously, painting eerie yellow-and-green pictures of what it sees, and storing the memory of those images in a bank of computer drums in Salt Lake City, Utah. The pictures are detailed. They show the position of each plane within the radar's arc of vision. If an aircraft carries a small black box called a transponder, its speed and direction are also recorded – and sometimes, when the pilot has fed the proper code into his instruments, the destination and purpose of its flight. GYVP, of course, would not have had such a sophisticated device on board, but from any two or more recordings of its presence, much could have been deduced. This procedure is called an ITAP – Interim Track Analysis Program – and it is a cumbersome one. To search even a small area of the sky for a time span as limited as ten minutes could require eight hours of painstaking examination of computer tapes. Even to institute an ITAP, Rauscher would need specific information. Furthermore, radar works only on lines of sight. Even if a tower were pointing its disc in the right direction at the right time, the plane they were looking for could have been hidden by a mountain peak or a heavy storm cloud.

The Cessna's last known location was Livingston, and its intended destination, Boise, was clear. But there were dozens of hidden and seldom used emergency landing strips on which it could have descended safely and, because of the mountains or through its own technical difficulties, not have been able to make radio contact.

With a disappointing response to the first two formal alerts, Rauscher fed his request for information into a still more intricate network: the small radio stations and the telephone systems of the back country. Please call, said the message he had issued, if you can tell us anything at all about a white Cessna 172 with black trim and the call letters C-GYVP, last seen at . . . and so on.

As was customary in the search and rescue methodology, the description of the plane was less than full. Like detectives working the city streets, people who practise SAR – Search and Rescue – have to deal constantly with the public's desire to be in on the action. The SAR net can bring in as much false information as true, so the sketchier the request, the easier it is to determine the accuracy of the response.

With the declaration of the search's launch, Rauscher had been in touch with his counterparts in two neighbouring states. Wyoming, far to the south of the presumed route, was not promising. But Montana, from Livingston to the Idaho border, was a distinct possibility, and Rauscher joined forces with his counterpart in Helena, the Montana State capital.

The man agreed upon by both the agencies to head the day-to-day operation, an operation that had to be designed from its conception to stretch into days and perhaps weeks, was Sam Griggs, a pilot and officer of the Montana SAR system whose skills and knowledge of the country were respected by aviators throughout the West. Griggs had been intrigued by everything about flying since he was a child. Polio had left his left leg almost useless, and he had had a battle even to be allowed to take his licence examination. But his scrappy and determined nature was hidden under a diplomatic manner he'd acquired in dozens of searches. He would be able to bear the tedium and the nerve-stretching involvement of friends and relatives who were sure to start arriving soon. Despite his crippled leg, he could fly as long and as well as any of the pilots he might be called upon to summon and command. Griggs would be their man.

As one of his first decisions, Griggs moved the headquarters of the search to Bozeman, Montana, inside the mountains. The weather was threatening, he reasoned, and one of the first places a storm could close down was the Livingston pass, which would isolate the town from the mountains. Since it was almost certain the plane was west of that pass – somewhere in the border area – best to hunker down behind it, and keep the search going west. The telephone number in the message that went out on the back country network was a Bozeman one, and calls were already coming in by Monday morning. But none of them, it seemed to the officials of the search, was as specific and promising as Les Hudson's.

The problem now was how to follow it up. If the plane Hudson had seen – and from his description it seemed probable, especially because of his own flying experience – was indeed GYVP, it was going in the wrong direction. Why would they so carefully ask directions from Livingston to Boise and then head off toward what could only, the searchers realized as they looked over the maps for possible alternative destinations, have been Yellowstone Park? Yellowstone was a scenic wonder, sure, but in this weather? Had anyone mentioned it in the airport at Livingston?

Yes, Glen Raney now recalled, someone had. The girl had mentioned Yellowstone. But they'd asked so *specifically* about getting to Boise. Surely they couldn't have changed their minds. There was that moment's pause on the runway. Had they decided then to go sightseeing? It seemed unlikely, but it would fit with Les Hudson's sighting. The clues were slim, but all they had to go on.

"Let's check it out down that way a bit," Rauscher suggested to Griggs.

The food supply that Brent and Donna had inventoried so carefully did not last long. The Smarties went first. Since Brent's jaw, with his teeth still hanging loose, made chewing impossible, he sucked each individual piece of candy-coated chocolate. Donna also savoured the sweet taste of each for as long as she could, telling herself lies about how much energy she was absorbing. The sunflower seeds left over from their second day soon followed, portioned out a few at a time over the days of waiting. Again, chewing was impossible for Brent, but he found he could suck on the seeds, too, and almost feel the nourishment. Once, Donna chewed a seed between her teeth, and with as much delicacy as she could muster passed the shreds over to Brent. He swallowed the morsel easily.

Modesty of any sort had left them. Although they seldom needed to urinate – once or twice a day was enough – they stopped their attempts to get out of the plane and relieved themselves through the cabin doors. Brent's urine remained dark, but the bright red that had been apparent in the Thermos cup faded.

They began to fantasize about food, and they spent hours describing to one another what they would eat when they returned to civilization. "Big mounds of fresh strawberries," one would say, and the other would add "whipped cream, about a quart of whipped cream. All thick and gooey and full of sugar." ... "Or maybe just a dish of ice cream." ... "With chocolate sauce." ... "One of those sundaes you can get at the Canada, with nuts and chocolate and a marshmallow." As they talked, they could *taste* the food, and they would plan even more elaborate menus each session, steaks and chops and dishes full of potatoes and green vegetables. They recalled fine meals they'd eaten before, and discussed the skills of Cindy and Evelyn as cooks. Instead of increasing their hunger, as they had feared when they first began them, their fantasy sessions would seem to satisfy it, but then they would be brought back swiftly to reality as one or the other would retch, and all that came from their stomachs was green and bitter bile.

On Thursday, their fifth day of isolation, they ripped out the left front seat, where Brent had been sitting during the flight. The floor beneath was solid with ice. They hacked at the ice with one of the seat's steel struts. They made two happy discoveries. The first was Brent's watch, torn from his wrist during the crash, still, incredibly, in working order under the seat. He set it to the date – May 10 – and to Donna's for the time. The second discovery gave them more immediate pleasure: an unopened bottle of Pepsi-Cola. They resolved to make it last as long as they could.

"But let's just have one sip now," Brent said. He opened it with the toy jackknife.

Donna put the bottle to her mouth and poured in just enough to feel the prickle of the bubbles and the nectar of the cold syrup.

Brent followed.

They looked at each other.

"One more," said Brent, going first and passing the bottle to Donna.

They couldn't stop. Back and forth went the bottle, each taking one swallow before handing it across the plane, slowly at first and then more quickly as the cola ran into their empty stomachs.

"That's the best Pepsi I've ever tasted in my life," Brent said.

Donna grinned at him sheepishly.

They finished the bottle. It took them half an hour.

Almost the same thing occurred following another – and for Brent, equally thrilling – double discovery. Under the dashboard, buried in the snow that now filled every corner of the cabin and which the fire couldn't melt, they found the package of cigarettes he'd opened Saturday morning and, treasure of treasures, a paper package of matches. There were seven cigarettes unsmoked and seven matches unlit.

"I'll just light one," Brent promised. Carefully, he drew a cigarette from the package and placed it between his blood-caked lips. He fumbled out a match and scratched it across the bottom of the folder. It flared. He cupped it to the cigarette and inhaled. As soon as he could feel the smoke in his mouth, he threw the match to the cabin floor. Even as he dragged the smoke of his first cigarette in five days into his lungs he looked down at the match he'd used. There was still some colour on its head – but not enough to light another smoke.

"Jesus, this is good," he said. He could feel the smoke biting into his lungs. "It's too bad you don't smoke; we could share this."

"I just wish we had another Pepsi."

"You think there are any more?"

"How many did we buy?"

"Just four, I think. We had those in the plane, eh? There was that can of Pepsi Norm had with him and ... I don't know. This is all, I'm sure."

"Mom told me not to buy too many. I wonder what she's thinking about now."

"*Jesus*, this cigarette tastes good," Brent said.

"How long do you think seven will last?"

"I don't care. I've got one now."

"You're coughing."

"Well, I haven't had a smoke for a long time. It feels like it's warming me."

72

"Go ahead."

He smoked it right to the end. When the butt was less than half an inch and his stiffened fingers could no longer hold it, he crushed it against the floor of the plane. Then:

"Donna?"

"Yes."

"I'll make you a deal."

"What?"

"I'm going to smoke them all."

"What do you mean?"

"I'll smoke all of them right now."

"What kind of deal is that?"

"Here's how I figure it. If I try to space these out, I'll be thinking of it all the time. Like, when can I have another cigarette? But if I don't have any, I just won't think about it. I haven't thought much about smoking since I thought these were lost."

"You've talked about it often enough."

"Yeah, well, I didn't know where they were. But if I smoke them now, they'll be gone, and I won't think about them."

"They're your cigarettes."

"Yeah, but they're not my matches, and right now the matches are worth more than the cigarettes, right?"

Donna didn't answer.

"Like, I figure the matches are ours, just like the clothes we split up are ours, and you've got the right to say if I can use them. So my deal is if you let me use one more match now I'll smoke them all."

"Now?"

"Now. I just want to use one more match. I'll even try to get another light off that first one. See where the colour's still on the head. But if I can't, then I'll use another one, and we'll have five left. Okay?"

"Sure. I guess so."

Brent nodded at her and then, one by one, he smoked the remaining six cigarettes in the package. The half burned match from his first light didn't work. He used a second, but from the light it provided he chainsmoked for an hour and a half, using each butt to ignite the next cigarette before stubbing it out on the floor. The smoking made him dizzy, but he was pleased with himself.

The last bit of food now left from their luggage was the granola bar that Cindy had packed for Brent. They saved it as long as they could.

The hunger was always with them, sometimes expressing itself just through a longing that resembled an emotion, but sometimes coming as pain, too. As early as Tuesday, well before the discovery of the last bottle of Pepsi, Brent's stomach cramps were severe enough to convince him he had either heartburn or an ulcer. At one point he was sure he had appendicitis, but Donna assured him his pain was located too high in his body for that. The pain was worse at night, and only water would soothe it. They worked out a system to give Brent water before they retired. On the upward slope of a snowbank just outside the plane, where they could reach it with their arms, they spread out the baby-blanket-sized piece of dark carpeting they had torn from the plane's floor. On top of that, a foot-square piece of metal from the torn wing. They shaped the metal into a rough V. Over it all, they threw fistfuls of snow, and below the whole assembly went the lid from Brent's shaving soap, to collect the run-off. Lidful by lidful, they would collect the water in a pop can, saving it for nightfall, when Brent would sip it to relieve his pain.

On Thursday afternoon the hunger was intolerable, and they decided to prepare the granola bar for eating. Donna acted as chef. She filled a Pepsi can with snow, melting it over the fire, and adding more and more snow until there was enough for her recipe. Using the top of the Thermos as a mixing bowl, she ground the granola bar into the water to make a thin gruel.

"This is terrible," she proclaimed.

"At least we can get it down. I don't even have to chew it."

"It's still terrible."

"You never were much of a cook."

"It's not *that* bad."

"I'll eat yours if you want."

They finished it. Donna was right. It tasted terrible.

And then, finally, the toothpaste. They squeezed inch long lines of it on their fingers and licked it off. It was, to their surprise, not unpleasant. It was sort of like eating mints, they decided.

That night, Thursday, there was nothing left to eat at all, and just as darkness closed over the canyon they saw the end of their fire.

Brent still had the five matches that remained from his session with the cigarettes, and the yellow lighter was still capable of throwing sparks, but the gas they'd been able to siphon from the valve in the wing was now gone, and no amount of jiggling with the coat hanger would yield more. Worse, they had burned everything flammable in the plane: the maps from Williston, the Kleenex, several of the air-sickness bags – even Brent's Bauer bag – and all that was loose in all their luggage, and which they couldn't wear. Donna's work book from school and Brent's flight log they kept more as symbols than as reserve fuel. Like the Kleenexes, the papers from their pages would have lasted only minutes at the most. The little fire burned itself out.

Throughout the days on the mountain, Donna felt a growing sense of guilt – although "guilt," even as she came to talk about her feelings to Brent, was not a word she used. "It's my fault," she would say when her spirits were at their lowest. "It's my fault that we're here, and that Dad's dead," and no amount of reassurance otherwise would convince her she was wrong.

It was the dog. Donna had had her heart set on a puppy of her own since the previous fall, when Frisky, the dog Brian had left at home for her to care for when he'd got married to Tara and moved into his own house, had died from old age. She could have one for a gradua-tion present, her parents had assured her, but she was impatient. She wanted a puppy. And one day at the school library where she'd been looking through a book about various breeds, she'd seen a picture of a West Highland Terrier and she'd known that was what she wanted: a Westie. She became something of a pest about it, in fact, but the family went along with her. By the time they were preparing their new custom van for a trip to California that winter, the Westie had become such a part of the Johnson lore that Don had an artist paint a picture of one on the inside of the van.

They'd almost picked up the dog on that same vacation to Califor-nia. The trip had been a good one, another memory for the family to cherish and to look forward to talking over in the future. Don and Evelyn, Brian and Tara, and one of Don's business associates and his wife, had gone down ahead, driving nonstop from Estevan to Utah. Then after thirty-six hours with the men driving in shifts – Don as always being the leader – they came out of the mountains at a favourite spot for the first golf of the season, and continued on to Las Vegas and California, combining, as the family so often did on their trips together (even this was hard to talk about now) business and pleasure. They stopped near Disneyland, and after a week or two the younger couples had flown home, and Donna and Brent and Cindy and the two Dyer kids had flown down to join Don and Evelyn.

Donna just wouldn't let up about the Westie, and when there was time, or when she could convince her mother to take her shopping, they'd scout the pet shops of California. Once she thought she'd found what she wanted – a perfect little male – in a Los Angeles pet shop window, but her mother had thought the price, $385, was too high, and wondered how the dog would handle the long trip home by van. Donna could wait.

On the way home, though, they'd stopped at a trailer park near Provo, Utah. Donna found a pay phone and checked the yellow pages for kennels and pet shops. She spent sixty cents in dimes without luck, until someone told her about a man named Dick Hannah in Draper, Utah, which was almost on the way home. Donna got her father and her father placed a call to Mr. Hannah. Mr. Hannah said yes, as it happened, he did know of a reliable breeder who, he was pretty sure, had a Westie pup for sale. His name was Jimmy Robertson, and he lived in Weiser, Idaho, about a hundred miles from Boise, but Mr. Robertson came into town a lot. In fact, Mr. Hannah said, it was too bad they were calling that day, because he happened to know Mr. Robertson was out of the state at the time. If he'd been at home, they probably would have picked up the dog right then. The young pup could have taken the drive from Idaho to – where was it? – Saskatchewan.

When the family got back from their holiday they called Mr. Robertson directly. They talked to him several times. He sent pictures. The pup and the price – $200 – were perfect. They made a deal.

During that series of telephone calls, Donna recalled now, they learned that Mr. Robertson had not in fact been out of the state when they'd called from the trailer park. Hannah had been confused over the dates. They could have picked the puppy up on their way home after all. "If only I'd found that out we wouldn't even have gone on this trip," Donna said bitterly, and nothing Brent could say would console her.

At first, when Donna slumped to her lowest, Brent would find himself wishing that, if he had to be alone in the mountains with someone – especially with a female – it could have been Cindy. He would imagine that the girl with him was not a girl, but a woman, *his* woman. But, as the days wore on and his reflections continued, he began to wonder if, after all, he'd have stayed alive even this long if indeed he'd been with his wife instead of his teenage sister-in-law; and finally, he did not wonder at all, but became convinced he wouldn't have survived. If it were Cindy, he told himself, he'd have been so busy worrying about her he'd have cared nothing for himself – not even taking his share of the Pepsi or the granola gruel. He'd have acted the husband, *made* her lean on him. With Donna, he was able to keep a kind of distance, to tell her to look after herself, in a way he couldn't imagine himself doing with his wife, so that, for example, when she fell into tears of guilt and self-pity as she told yet again the story of how they might have picked the dog up in the van, he could give in to his anger. "For Christ's sake, Donna," he would say – as he would probably not have been able to with Cindy. And often this instinctive reaction would snap Donna out of her tears in a way that sympathy might not have done.

Besides which, Donna was showing surprising strength. There were the tears, sure, but there were moments when she was almost . . . taking charge. She'd pulled the carpet up, he recalled; she'd figured out how to make the gruel; she'd made him take Don's coat. And maybe even more important, he found himself able to open up with her, to show his own weakness in a way he might have been reluctant to do with his wife. Funny, he thought, how he could open up more with someone he'd always thought of as just a little kid than he'd ever really been able to do with Cindy. Not that they didn't talk things over, but when they did it was always as husband and wife. Cindy had seen him cry, sure; he'd cried after that awful New Year's eve when he'd got into the booze and had the fight with Brian, and he'd had to get her not to leave him and God knows she'd seen him at his worst. But here in the cold and the terrifying quiet of the mountains he found himself able to weep not in penitence or to seek forgiveness, but just out of rage and sorrow and, yes, if you wanted to know the truth, out of a self-pity that wasn't any different from Donna's.

One night, early on, he'd reached a point where he just couldn't stand it any more. All he wanted was five minutes – five *minutes*, for God's sake – when there'd be no pain, and when the taste of bile and blood would leave his mouth, when he would be warm. He'd just wanted to quit, to sink into darkness along with Don, and he'd said so. But then Donna, little Donna, had told *him* to hold on, that they could make it, that they had to make it, and he'd snapped out of it. They were like two pistons, he thought, a two-piston engine. When one was down the other was up, and together they were putting out a power that, by God, was going to get them out of this. Yes, that was it, a two-piston engine, and the fuel they were running on was their love of God.

They were praying a lot now. The Lord's prayer. They must have said it a million and a half times. They'd say it during their nightly bedding-down ritual and in the mornings when they woke up. Just lie there and say the prayer, not to each other, but to God. They'd look at each other but each knew that their words were going to the Lord.

Chapter Six

For all the available technology, the process of search and rescue remains a very human game, a board game played for the highest conceivable stakes, and the most powerful pieces the strategists can deploy remain the small aircraft that are available to fly them over the area of the search. Pilots know this, and in country that is as wild as the mountains of Idaho and Montana they band together to offer their services as quickly and efficiently as they can. The next plane that is lost, they are all aware, could be their own. Willingly, they pay the penny-per-gallon surcharge of the fuel they use to keep the SAR organization ready. And when the call goes out, they come forward with their planes. Their time is donated. They can be reimbursed for the fuel they burn, if they remember to ask.

Each state has been carefully divided into a grid of rectangles measuring 128 square miles. Each rectangle is numbered, and for each the system designates one or more pilots. When the system is geared up, every square mile of a state can be flown at least once in a matter of a few days. This is the *grid* search, it is the foundation of SAR. The *route* search sends aircraft over the possible patterns the target plane may have flown, and can wend its way across parts of various rectangles in the grid.

The task of the search masters is to deploy their men and material in both these systems in the most useful manner. Besides the search from the air, they can scout the land by wheeled vehicles or, when the landscape becomes too wild, by foot or on horseback. Unable to use every method to search every valley and meadow and riverpath and mountain pass, the search masters must constantly choose among probabilities. And in the first hours and days of the search for GYVP, Worthie Rauscher and Sam Griggs and their colleagues conferred almost continually by radio and telephone, trying to narrow down the probabilities and, as best they could, eliminate rectangles and routes so as to make the most of the resources and the manpower at their disposal.

By mid-week, as Brent and Donna huddled inside the cabin of GYVP, there was almost more help in Bozeman than the search masters could use.

More than thirty people had come from Canada. Brian led the contingent of Johnsons, followed and accompanied by Don's brother Keith, who'd been the host on their Uranium City hunting trip, and Keith's daughter Cheryl and her husband Bob McLaughlin. Ron Coulter, Donna's boyfriend, left school to come to Bozeman. Jack Sweeney, married to Evelyn's sister Joey, took time off from his production job at the Regina *Leader-Post*. Mel Grimes, a nephew of Evelyn's who had known Brent since Brent's emergence as a purveyor of scorched golf balls to the Johnson's family – Mel's father had always suspected arson – flew down in his own plane. So did Brock Perry, who had first met Brent as a three-year-old who rode a tricycle in front of Perry's car. Former business associates of Don's – Ray Madden, from Red Deer, Alberta, and Jim Worthington of Williston – found time to come down, as did Garth Mullan, assistant fire chief in Estevan and a veteran of arctic SAR, and Craig Dyer, no relation of Brent's, and Jack Muirhead, a hunting partner. All of them were frightened, as much by their lack of knowledge of what had happened to their friends and relatives as by their growing certainty that the plane was down. They wanted to *do* something.

Sharon Pischke arrived with Norm's brother Walter and Dale Gross, a prosperous farmer from the Gravelbourg area who'd employed Norm to spray his crops and whose brother was a cabinet minister in Saskatchewan's socialist government.

Among the first to arrive was Bob Larter, a big jovial farm implement dealer who represented Estevan as a Conservative in the provincial legislature. Politics? "Sure," Larter said. "There were four constituents in that plane." But one of them, Brent, had also been a classmate of Larter's son Bob, Jr., and Norm had been Larter's pilot.

There was more to it than politics. Sometimes Sam Griggs thought they'd just tilted the Canadian prairie and let the people slide south.

Sam didn't know what to do with them all. His grid search was proceeding slowly. The snow that had started on Saturday afternoon kept falling intermittently and reduced both flying opportunities and visibility. But more and more sections of the maps he'd tacked up in his office at Flite Line Service at the Bozeman airport were being coloured in. Because of the changing snow conditions, some of the rectangles had to be flown more than once. But to keep his search planes as manoeuvrable as possible in the mountain passes, he wanted only one observer per plane. "You'll have to look in as many directions as you can," he would tell them. "And don't use your binoculars until you think you see something. Otherwise you're just restricting your field of vision."

Sometimes he wished he had a fleet of snowmobiles and could send a posse of Canadians fanning out on route searches, but the snow was too thick for that even if it had been possible. He could use them as drivers, though; many had brought their cars, and when there was a lead that could be checked out on the ground, they were more than willing to run out for him.

Even for the SAR veterans, the work was tiring: hour after hour of straining your eyes to pick out a sign, *any* sign, from the blazing white of the mountainsides, or the trees that stood, as Mike Ferguson of the Montana division said, "like hairs on a dog's back." The pilots would come back to Bozeman each night to fill in their flight logs for the day, or call the data in: departure point, method of navigation, check points covered, legs flown, landing time. The stacks of paper records grew. The maps on the wall grew darker as the rectangles were coloured in.

The logs of the search masters measured the rhythm of the search, the terse shorthand of Rauscher and Griggs disguising the rise and fall of their emotions, the frustrations of the weather, the flickers of false hopes, the leads that looked like leads and then ... petered out.

IDAHO: MAY 6:

0925   Search declared.

0945   Col. Nicholson [from Scott Air Force Base] – has every reason to believe that acft is down.

1000   Briefing completed. CAP [Civil Air Patrol] being initiated.
        Montana also pursuing.

MONTANA:

1025   Call for Wx [weather briefing] ... mod to severe turbu-
        lence ...
1100   Called Idaho. They have talked w/Scott.
1105   Called Jack. He will call tower to check on comm, field
        check.
1110   Called Jack. We will both go to work to run search.
1120   At wx [weather] bureau to check on route.
1130   At work ...

IDAHO:

1145   Received a call from Brian Johnson (son of one party on
        missing a/c) ... He will call back in about 3 hours.
1215   West Yellowstone ramp check negative.
1218   Asked Army guard to check emergency airstrips enroute to
        Boise.
1220   Wx still bad at ... Monida Pass – will launch as soon as
        weather permits.

MONTANA:

1240   IDA SAR called .... They are going to get a/c to search
        Monida Pass [near Livingston, and on the route Raney had
        suggested] ... Wx permitting. Said a Brian Johnson called
        from SASK ... IDA also said can send two [Cessna] 182s
        down tomorrow. Worthie Rauscher said mod-sev/turbul in
        S.E. Idaho yesterday.

These notations were for Sunday, May 6, the first real day of the
search. Already the rectangles that looked most promising were being
checked off. Each rectangle was now being divided into quadrants,
lettered from A to D. Each quadrant was twenty-seven square miles.

IDAHO:

1245   IF [Idaho Falls] CAP will cover emergency strips .... Also
        roads. TWF [Twin Falls] ... will cover 136D, 137, 139,

140, 169, 170, 171, 172. BOI will cover 100, 101CD, 102, part of C, 132B, 133 n. of freeway, 134, 135, 165B, 166ABD, 167, 168ACD.

The weather that was restricting the search, and at the same time billowing around the lost Canadians, was bitter. Winds were reported at up to sixty knots in the mountains, and the temperatures at 10,000 feet and above were as low as ten below zero Fahrenheit.

IDAHO: MAY 7:
0730   1 acft airborne. 3 more will be ready shortly.

MONTANA:
0730   Andy Morris called. Has 3 acft out. He will go out in a few minutes. Should be four on search.
0754   Called Jack Martinelli. He has 2 acft in air.

IDAHO:
1155   Jean Sieber (F). Idaho Falls. 2 planes back from grids 22 & 24, saw nothing, new snow on ground ... weather deteriorating rapidly.
1255   Merrill called all crews down – searched 19, 20, 21, 51, 52, 56 and 57. All negative.

MONTANA: MAY 8:
0830   Maj. [Duane] Cocking and one other driving into Yellowstone Valley to contact people personally.

And so it went, day after day, hour after dreary hour. Hopes up – a shiny object seen on a hill above a dam (Idaho, May 8, 0840) – hopes down: there was nothing there (May 9, 0910: ground search was negative).

On each plane that flew was a check-listed survival package, neatly stored in a metal box, that offered a silent and constant reminder of what the passengers of GYVP, if they were still alive, did *not* have: spare blankets, nylon rope, fish-hooks, candles, a saw, a signal mirror, flashlight, canned heat, a compass, a can opener, and food: candy, bouillon cubes, tea, salt, chocolate and peanut-butter food sticks, raisins, cocoa, instant broth and beef jerky. In addition, nearly all the planes carried firearms for hunting. These men knew the mountains.

Norm, it was now evident, did not.

"Hadn't he ever flown in here?" pilot after pilot would ask.

"Never," they would be told.

"Jesus Christ."

Throughout the first days of the search, the nagging possibility remained that the party had changed their minds either in the air or on the runway at Livingston and decided to head south for Yellowstone. Les Hudson's sighting of the "blue" and white Cessna could be neither proved nor disproved. Other people – three of them in one day alone – reported equally possible sightings; none of them proved out. The most promising came from a group of five fishermen who had been spread out along the banks of the Yellowstone River on Saturday afternoon. One of them was a pilot with almost as many hours in his log as Norm himself. He and two others had seen a plane, they said, which could very well have been the missing Skyhawk; all five of the party had heard it. Where was it going? The fishermen couldn't guess. They had seen it approach a bank of clouds and then turn around, as if heading back toward Livingston. The ground search along the banks of the river was intensified. Nothing. The clues were running out. The "sickle" had been covered as closely as it could be flown. There was nothing to do but fly it again – and keep checking the rectangles on the grid around it.

If only, Sam Griggs said time and time again, they could put themselves in Norm Pischke's place. What had been on his mind? Where could he have gone?

In Estevan, Jimmy Dyer rose alone, as always, at 5:30 in the morning, well before the pale prairie dawn. His wife Evylene slept. Jimmy was and is a remarkable man. Marked strongly by the Depression years – during most of which he served as a jack of all newspaper trades on the town's weekly *Mercury* – and by his own frustration at being unable to do anything but push paper during the Second World War, he married into the family that owned Estevan's Ford dealership and, after his father-in-law's death, changed its name to Dyer Ford. Largely through his own energy and determination, Jimmy built Evylene's father's business into one of Estevan's most thriving enterprises, expanding not only the Ford dealership but the used-car operation as well. He was a compulsive worker, a tough boss but a fair one, always the first to work and always ready to chew out, in language that belied his own regular church-going habits, any of his employees who lagged on the job or were late. "There are sixteen men working here," he bellowed one day. "And if all of them are five minutes late that's eighty goddamn minutes I've lost – one hour and twenty minutes. At nine dollars an hour that's twelve goddamn dollars. With mark-up, that's twenty dollars I've lost. In five minutes! Let the sons of bitches get here on time. I do!"

Jimmy is a small man, just over five foot five, who wears his thinning grey hair cut short. Wire-rimmed glasses perch on his nose. His temper bristles close to the surface. He is something of a town character. People imitate him by yelling loudly and swearing a lot, but he is universally respected. He has held high office on or in everything from the town council to the Masons and, a rare honour for a Protestant, the Catholic hospital board. There is a Dyer Road in the most prestigious part of town. He is a man of deep convictions and deep prejudices; he will blister any bureaucrat who so much as casts a shadow on the business he has built up, and he was so unforgiving of the sins of his own father that he refused to go to his funeral. He is also a man capable of deep and abiding love. For the past twenty-five years much of that love had been steadfastly directed at his second child and only son, Brent.

For the first eighteen years of his life, Brent returned that love with a figurative thumb to his nose. When he was twelve, Brent stole Jimmy's coin collection and, with a friend, took off for Vancouver. The two boys hitchhiked as far as Swift Current, almost 200 miles to the west, then cashed the coin collection for bus fare to the coast. Jimmy, having heard his son brag about where he'd go if he ever had the money, called the Vancouver police, and the boys were met at the bus station and taken into custody. When they returned, Jimmy forgave Brent and told him that some day he would have to repay the money he'd stolen.

The transgressions continued. In his first year of high school, Brent got into a brawl with the principal at a school dance. Brent was drunk at the time. He broke into stores for money for booze. In a larger community, Brent would have been a "juvenile delinquent," worried over by social workers and the courts. In Estevan, he was just a bad-assed kid, and Jimmy continued to support him. Friends of the family would urge Jimmy to do something to curb his son. "I can't," he would reply. "Besides, what is there to do? He's my flesh and blood."

When Brent was seventeen, Jimmy suffered a heart attack. Everyone who knew the Dyers blamed it on Brent's wildness. While Jimmy was in the hospital, one friend of the family asked Brent to help with some household repairs. When he had the youngster alone, he threatened to kick the tar out of him if he didn't straighten up. Sure, said Brent. But the threat was ignored. Ten days after his heart attack, Jimmy went back to work at the Ford agency.

The next year Jimmy, who had developed diabetes following his heart attack, found the note from Brent announcing his intention to marry. Jimmy helped arrange the wedding. He made the down payment on the house for them; it was more than Jimmy had ever taken from the Ford agency in a year. He said he'd look after the monthly payments. In his office desk, unbeknownst to Evylene, he still kept the runaway note.

When the law finally caught up with Brent and he was sent to Regina to do his time, Jimmy was the first to drive the 200 prairie miles to see him. He took money, in case Brent needed it for cigarettes in jail. Brent didn't, he said, but he took the money anyway. Jimmy drove back home that night.

Now, in the kitchen of his house, Jimmy spread his breakfast out before him: toast, a piece of cheese, one pill for his heart condition, one for his diabetes. The kettle bubbled on the stove. Jimmy bowed his head.

"Oh Lord," he prayed in silence, "bring back my son from his troubles. Let him be all right again."

Chapter Seven

His teeth would have to come out. There was the pain, of course, but worse than the pain as the days wore on was the infection working its way into his gums and the shattered bone of his jaw. It was running pus, so thickly that Brent could spit it out, although spitting itself was difficult, since it meant hitting the broken lower teeth with his tongue. It added to the sour taste that lingered in the back of his mouth. He could never quite clear his throat.

On Friday, when they had been on the mountain six days, he began to work at one of the lower cuspids with his fingers. It was hardly attached at all. It came out easily. Then another tooth, and another. They came out like weeds, except there were nerves in the roots. Once he almost passed out. But he kept at it, working the forefingers of his hands like pliers, and on one occasion digging right around a tooth with the point of the toy knife, slicing into his own flesh.

Donna watched in horror.

"Doesn't it hurt?" she asked.

"You're goddamn right it hurts," Brent said, except the words came out muffled: "Ure ott amm rye it urr."

He settled back into his corner of the cabin. The effort had exhausted him. He gathered the teeth in one hand and stared at them. He found a piece of Kleenex and wrapped them in it. Then he put the package in his pocket.

"I'm taking these back to Geoffrey," he said. "I'm going to put them under his pillow when we get back there and when he wakes up the next morning he's going to get the biggest tooth-fairy present in the history of Estevan."

Donna was getting stronger. By Saturday, the end of their first full week on the mountain, there was still little feeling in her feet, but she was able to pull one shoe, her left, over the swelling. With that, and a moccasin she'd fashioned from the torn carpeting on her right foot, she was able to move around. She grew more adventurous, although she still could not move comfortably; she was still a prisoner of pain and exhaustion.

The storm, which had abated on Tuesday and blown itself out by Wednesday, had left the plane covered in snow and had piled drifts against its uphill side. Hopping and hobbling, Donna was able to brush some of the thickest snow from the top of the wings. The more she pushed away, the angrier she became; the wings were white, and without markings and from above, she realized, the plane would be invisible against the snow. She remembered the bright orange aircraft she'd seen between Williston and Livingston.

Still angry, she started pushing the snow from the side of the fuselage, uncovering as best she could the two black stripes that ran backwards to the door and then became one solid strip, into which the Cessna's call letters were set in white. If an aircraft flew by low enough, they might see that, she thought. She moved to the tail. Snow had blown against the rudder, but even in her condition it was fairly easy to knock it off and expose the trademark of the Skyhawk. The symbol was painted in gold, but against the white paint, it appeared faint and dim.

Gathering firewood remained beyond her. Tantalizingly close to the plane – perhaps fifty feet away – small evergreens thrust upward through the snow, but she was as unable to move across the heavy drifts to tear at their branches as she would have been to shinny up the side of the dead hardwood that the wing had hit, and which now loomed up behind them. They would have to do without fire.

Brent, meanwhile, had begun experimenting with the fire extinguisher they'd found inside the cabin. After some fiddling, he managed to get it to squirt a visible gas. Now unnecessary for protection in the flameless cabin, it nevertheless might serve as a signal. He soon found that by aiming it through the broken window he could send puffs of what appeared to be smoke into the air.

"I'm going to save it," he said, "so that if someone flies over I can at least show them there's something alive down here."

"Will someone come?"

"Sure. How many stories have you heard about people who've been picked up by search planes? They know we're missing. They must be looking. They'll find us."

"I can hold on."

"Sure, we both can."

"God wants us to live."

"God and Don. You've got to think about the coat. Your dad gave you the coat. He knew he was going to die, but he wanted you to live. You've *got* to live."

"So do you."

This had become, by Saturday, a litany, as if when their own strength waned they would draw not only upon God but upon their certain knowledge of Don's sacrifice on their behalf, and they would use that knowledge to gird themselves against the cold and the pain and the constant hunger, all of which brought them to the most difficult decision either of them had ever made.

The last of their provisions, even the toothpaste, was gone. There was no sign of Norm, and by mid-week their hopes of his having found help and returning to them had faded. Hope of being spotted from the air, in spite of their brave talk of past rescues, was almost as faint. Without food, they could not last much longer.

Now, on Saturday, their choice seemed clear to them: they would have to eat something or they would die. All that was left to satisfy their hunger was Don's body. They would have to eat of its flesh.

Each of them had seen, and been moved by, the movie *Survive!*, the story of the survivors of a plane crash in the Andes in 1972, the same story as told in Piers Paul Read's *Alive*. Now, although it was not the kind of movie they discussed at the time it played Estevan, they found themselves referring to it. The Andes survivors, it seemed to them, had faced realistically the same choice they now had: a choice between dealing with their own revulsion at the idea of consuming human flesh, on the one hand, and, on the other, perishing from cold and starvation on the mountain side. Their own feelings about the young South Americans portrayed in the film were that they had chosen, logically and inevitably, in favour of life. If anything, the South Americans had seemed more heroic to them for coming to grips with their disgust than they would have seemed if they'd succumbed to their fate. Had they been punished? The movie didn't make it clear, but that, surely, was beside the point. It was how *they* had felt about it just as it was how Brent and Donna would feel about it now, and how the God, who was so real to them, would feel about it, that mattered. Most importantly, the two young people were certain they had Don's blessing, made so clear to them by his giving of the coat to Donna. If he had been willing to give his *life* so that she might live, then surely his spirit would not mind if they took of his body. He would *want* them to.

"Your dad is watching us, Donna," Brent said. "He's watching over us just the way God is, and right now he's saying, 'I hope they eat that old body down there, because it's no use to me. I've left it.'"

Brent was confident he could do the butchery. He'd been around raw meat as long as he could remember. He'd taken his first shot at a duck (and missed) when he was six, and helped to clean the day's shoot at home. He'd shot his first deer before he was in his teens, and cut out the meat himself. The summer he was thirteen his best friend was Mark Newton, with whom he'd run to Vancouver carrying the stolen coin collection. Mark's father owned the town packing plant and had given the boys work, cleaning fowl and boning out the carcasses of animals for sausages. It had been easy work for a hunter. The toughest part was killing the geese, which farmers brought live to the packing plant. But Brent had figured out a way to bend coat hangers to make a kind of leg-snare, and he would trap the geese and slit their throats as quickly as any of the older workers. When duck season opened that fall, he and Mark began cutting classes to work at the packing plant. Hunters – Americans, mostly – would bring in their day's kill for cleaning and dressing. The Americans weren't very good hunters. They'd show up with small gadwalls and teal and widgeons, "shit ducks," the boys would call them, the kind you could get close to town. The boys would tease the visiting hunters, but if they took the teasing well they'd tell them where the big juicy mallards were, down south of Oungre, or near the Torquay bridge. And then the hunters would bring their bigger trophies back for cleaning, and wink at the boys in secret thanks. Sure, Brent could cut the flesh.

Except he couldn't.

Don's feet and ankles, the parts of him that had been nearest the fire, were almost roasted, but that's still what they were, parts of Don.

"We've got to pray," Brent told Donna.

"He'd have wanted us to do this," she assured him.

"I'll do it."

"Let's pray."

He put down the pocket knife. In the cramped cabin, they knelt over the body. "Our Father," they began, and together they went through the comforting words yet again. "Forgive us our trespasses," they said, "as we forgive them that trespass against us."

"We've got to ask the Lord," said Donna. "We've got to ask Him if it's the right thing to do, and we'll feel His answer in our hearts."

The idea of cannibalism is much closer to the surface of Western life than most people realize. Johnny Carson makes jokes about it ("During a wedding ceremony of cannibals it is customary for the groom to kiss the bride and munch on the best man"). Cannibal humour appears in small magazines ("How do you like your mother-in-law?" "Well done."); in cartoons of small men with big lips and bones through their noses and on bumper stickers ("Rugby players eat their dead"*). Images of the consumption of human flesh permeate our slang of work – "He'll chew your ass out for that" – and even of our sexual practices. But in spite of the familiarity with which we mention cannibalism, very few of us understand even our own attitudes toward it.

In the spring of 1979, at almost precisely the time that Brent and Donna were facing their dreadful decision, a debate that had begun two years earlier was flaring up, among other places, on the pages of *The New York Times* and in the influential *New York Review of Books*.

* One wonders if the people who sport this jolly slogan on their way to North American rugby games are aware of its grisly origins. Many of the survivors of the Andes crash of 1972, who ate the flesh of some of their dead teammates, were in fact members of a Uruguayan rugby team.

Although the debate was as far from the young couple's consciousness as its participants, most of whom sat in the warm offices of eastern U.S. universities, were from their frigid aerie, the questions the academics were dealing with were exactly those Brent and Donna were trying to sort out: questions of the morality of cannibalism, and of the attitudes and mental programming that civilized – or presumably civilized – people of the twentieth century would bring to bear on the choice Brent and Donna were being forced to make.

At the heart of the debate was the brilliant American anthropologist Marvin Harris. In a book called *Cannibals and Kings*, published in 1977, Harris had offered a challenging analysis of why some societies have condoned the eating of human flesh and why, having done so, they stopped. He suggested that the causes of both actions, starting and stopping, were not so much spiritual as economic, and that humankind was capable not only of eating the flesh of its own species, but of harvesting it like beef cattle. Not only were humans capable of such an action, he argued, but they had done so on at least one occasion and on a monumental scale.

Harris's principal evidence was the case of the Aztecs, at whose capital, Tenochtitlan, the Spanish had found evidence of as many as 136,000 people killed and eaten. And, Harris said, "All edible parts were used in a manner strictly comparable to the consumption of the flesh of domesticated animals. . . . The Aztec priests can legitimately be described as ritual slaughterers in a state-sponsored system geared to the production and redistribution of substantial amounts of animal protein in the form of human flesh."

Tough stuff. Critics responded equally vigorously. To argue, they said, that cannibalism had been committed by the Aztecs only "to get some meat" was a case of looking at the world as an extension of "western business utilitarianism." The Aztec killings were not answers to a practical need, but *rituals*. "It was not cannibalism. It was the highest form of communion," wrote Marshall Sahlins of the University of Chicago. "Of all the peoples in the hemisphere who practised intensive agriculture, the Aztecs probably had the greatest natural protein resources."

In the spring of 1979, Marvin Harris was back in the fray, this time with a book called *Cultural Materialism*. He repeated his arguments about the Aztecs. He expanded on them. The facts of Aztec life were, he said, that from 1500 B.C. to 1500 A.D. the Valley of Mexico, where the Aztecs had dwelt, had been fished and hunted out, and to assume that the 1,500,000 people who lived there could be fed from the available wild meat was "worth about as much as the suggestion that New York City would get its meat from deer captured in the Catskills."

Why had the Aztecs stopped? Not through any spiritual conversion, Harris argued, but because of common practical sense. "Not only was the eating of prisoners of war a great waste of manpower, but it was the worst possible strategy for any state that had imperial ambitions. ... Cannibalism and empire don't mix ... to opt for a cannibal kingdom is to opt for perpetual war with one's neighbours and for a revolt-ridden realm in which people are literally treated as being good for nothing but stew meat." The decline of cannibalism among the Aztecs, in other words, was as practical and non-mystical a matter as its rise. When their society, however uniquely, had found it prudent to treat human beings as a source of nourishment it had done so. When the practice became less prudent, it had ceased.

Harris's critics also went back to the original information. There *had* been other sources of protein in the Valley of Mexico. Furthermore, as an entry in the *American Anthropologist* had pointed out as long ago as 1970, human flesh is not an efficient nutrient. "While [it] may serve as an emergency source of both protein and calories," the article said, "it is doubtful that regular people-eating ever had much nutritional meaning." No, even the Aztecs had committed cannibalism for reasons less easily established than their materialistic needs.

The more the arguments unfolded, the more clear became the reason why those involved felt so passionately. At the base of their academic disagreement was, and is, a difference of viewpoint about the very essence of human nature.

The most troubling question about human cannibalism may very well be not why we have practised it, but why we haven't practised it more often. As a species, we have no *instinctive* reluctance to eat the flesh of our own kind, and our decision not to do so is no less arbitrary or more natural than the squeamishness some of us feel about eating cattle or swine or insects or snakes, each of which others of us relish, or than the refusal of the French to eat broccoli. There are signs of cannibalism – charred human bones, skulls split to spill the brains – that predate history. "Peking man," wrote the anthropologist Konrad Lorenz, "the Prometheus who first learned to preserve fire, used it to roast his brothers: beside the first traces of the regular use of fire lie the mutilated and roasted bones of Sinanthropus pekinensis himself."

The word *cannibalism* itself, a mutation of *Carib*, came into European use after Columbus reported that the natives of the islands he'd first reached in the New World ate their prisoners. (Less well known, and less comfortably dwelt upon, is the fact that from the Carib word *babricot* we get our "barbecue"; a *babricot* was a grill of green boughs on which the Caribs roasted their prisoners.) But two centuries before Columbus, Marco Polo had told of anthropophagous acts he'd heard of in his travels to exotic lands, and long before *that* historians as venerable as Herodotus had written of their existence.

Cannibalism spanned the known world. In the exhaustive bibliography she prepared for Richard Cunningham's *The Place Where The World Ends*, yet another examination of the case that prompted Piers Paul Read's *Alive*, Carolyn Nelson found examples on virtually all continents and from virtually all races: the Tibetans of the first post-Christian century, the Cocomas of Peru, the Issidones of southeast Russia, the Basegu of Uganda, the Kwakiutl of North America.

The strand that held all these examples together, however, was that almost all of them were ritualistic, sacramental in character. The Tibetans thought their own bowels would make a better resting place for their dead parents than the cold ground. The Cocomas swallowed the bones of their dead relatives ground up in fermented drinks for much the same symbolic reason. The Issidones mixed the flesh of their fathers with that of sacrificed cattle. The Basegu *honoured* their dead by eating them; and for the Kwakiutl of the western Canadian coast, the biting and swallowing of flesh from living members of the tribe was a rite of male passage.

These were examples of endophagy, cannibalism within the tribe. And as long as there was a ritual base to the practice, other societies were able to comprehend it. Similarly with exophagy: if one ate one's fallen enemies to absorb their strengths, as did, for example, cannibal tribes of New Guinea, the Congo, and Cochin-China, it was somehow understandable. However pagan, it was a sacrament. Human.

European culture, moreover, had a parallel. Since 1215, when Pope Innocent III had made it a part of doctrine, Roman Catholics had regarded the bread and wine of the mass as the literal body and blood of Christ. This is the dogma of transubstantiation, and it may help to explain one of the most curious facts about Western society's attitude toward cannibalism: Alone among practices that were accepted and sometimes even encouraged by "primitive" cultures but rejected and deplored in the "civilized" world, from incest to female infanticide and even blatant sexual promiscuity, cannibalism has been neither banned by law nor forbidden by religion. It is, simply, not against our laws to eat one's neighbour, as if we have realized that the possibility is so remote that we won't even rule on it. To have outlawed it, indeed – and perhaps not incidentally – would have been to tell Roman Catholics that if what they had believed since the thirteenth century was true, they were breaking the law each Sunday morning.

There was another form in which cannibalism was accepted: necessity. If you *had* to, you could. European and American literature of exploration, famine, and survival is studded with instances of people eating the bodies of their dead: from the shipwrecked sailors on the Indian Ocean, to the Donner party of the early American West, or the starving wretched of the Nazi concentration camps, from the Uruguayan youths who were trapped in the Andes to – only weeks later but in a much less publicized event – the Canadian arctic pilot Martin Hartwell, who ate the flesh of a dead nurse when his plane went down in the Northwest Territories. How many events of the opposite kind there have been – of people who, faced with a choice between cannibalism and death, chose death – can't, for self-evident reasons, ever be known. Yet without exception we have welcomed back into the mainstream those who have chosen cannibalism over death. Society understands. The consumption of human flesh, said the American Jesuit Richard McCormick, in reflecting on the Andes incident for the *Washington Post*, is the moral equivalent of a heart transplant.

There are two boundaries to our tolerance. The first is murder.

Thou shall not kill, we say, even to eat – or, perhaps, *especially* to eat. There are few crimes more repugnant to civilized society than, to take one example, the case of Maria Hernandez, a Chilean who in 1942 killed her husband, dismembered his body and served pieces in her *empanadas* to the neighbours. Mrs. Hernandez was sent to a hospital for the criminally insane. In many parts of the "primitive" world too, the person who killed for meat was an aberration. No creature was more feared by the Algonkian Indians of northeastern Canada than the Windigo, a tree-sized spirit who roamed the woods, moaning through his lipless mouth, and searching for humans to clutch to his heart of ice. The Windigo had powers of possession; he could turn his victims into cannibals, and once an Algonkian was possessed and had tasted of human flesh he became an anathema to the tribe. He had to be killed. The second of our boundaries is pleasure. You may taste of the meat, but you must not like it. That the cannibals of New Guinea killed for revenge was understandable. That they said they enjoyed it was not. Long pig, they called it. So they were savages, and less than human.

But within those boundaries, our intellectual arguments falter. The intellect is not enough. The question is of the spirit. Our refusal to eat human flesh is much more than a refusal to increase the possibilities that others will eat us; it is part of our humanity, part of what links us with what we call divine. And so, too, can be our exceptions to our own rule, as the taking of communion is an expression of a spiritual love of the flesh that is consumed. We can consume what we love because we love it; the consumption is a matter of the soul, and only the soul can understand it.

With a prayer, Brent began to cut the flesh.

Chapter Eight

Down the carpeted hall, Cindy could hear the boys chattering reveille. It must be Brent's turn to get up. She reached out a languid arm. He wasn't there. Oh God, he still wasn't there. Eight days now, eight nights without him, longer than they'd ever been apart since the wedding. Still, the anger was there. Why didn't he *call*? He couldn't be missing. Well, missing, sure, but he must be somewhere. He couldn't be dead. Not her Brent. He wouldn't let it happen. He couldn't. Brock Perry had said the same thing when he'd called from Montana, and Brock was a pilot. He'd know. And he knew Brent. They had coffee together nearly every day. "If anyone's going to walk out of there, Cindy, it will be Brent Dyer," Brock had said.

Tuesday had been the worst day. She hadn't even known till noon on Monday when she got that call from Candice Bacham, her neighbour.

"Cindy? Oh, Cindy, I thought it was you."

"Who?"

"In the plane crash."

"Crash?"

"No, I didn't mean that. I meant missing. In the missing plane."

"Candice, what do you ...?"

"It was on the news, about the plane being missing. And all I heard was Dyer and Johnson, and something about a woman, and I thought it was you. Who is it? Is it Donna?"

Yes, it was Donna, she'd said, and she hadn't wanted to tell Candice this was the first she'd known they were calling the plane missing. That was so like Mom, and Brian too. They'd come over to her place on Sunday. To play cards, they'd said. But they didn't seem to have their minds on the game. And every time she'd tried to talk about Brent not having called, they'd changed the subject. "Must be hung up somewhere," Brian had said. Twenty-one years old, with two kids of her own, and they still treated her like a child.

But that was Sunday. Tuesday had been the worst.

Geoff had come home from school in tears.

"Is Daddy dead?" he'd asked.

"No, Geoffy, Daddy isn't dead."

"I knew it."

"Why? What's wrong?"

"Show and tell."

"What about show and tell?"

"Two of the kids had this story from the paper. It was about Daddy. It said his plane wasn't coming back."

"Of course it's coming back, Geoff."

"Where's my Daddy?"

"He's just stopped somewhere down in the United States, where they went to get Aunt Donna's dog, remember?"

"When's he coming home?"

"Soon, Geoffy, soon."

"Mommy?"

"Yes?"

"I don't like show and tell."

Today was Mother's Day. Brent always brought her ... it was no time to think about that. She'd be going to her parents' house later on. They'd all be there, Aunt Joey and Aunt Marie and maybe Grandma and Grandpa Johnson. She had some presents. A Rumoli set for her mother, and some smaller stuff for the others. Maybe they could play Rumoli. It would take their minds off their worries.

She needed her family. There were some things they didn't talk about, the Johnsons, but they were always there. Like when she'd had Geoffrey. The pains had started at three in the morning. Brent's licence was still suspended and she was too young to have one at all, so they'd called her dad. It seemed like only a couple of minutes before he was there, with his pyjama collar sticking out from under his sweater and needing a shave, but the Lincoln was warm outside the door and he was ready to go, without a word of complaint. She wondered if Brent would ever be like that. No, Brent would gripe. Brent griped about everything, even when he did it with a smile. They couldn't be more different, really, her quiet, steady, dependable father and the restless, spirited man she'd married. But they seemed to get along with each other – now. Maybe even liked each other, which was really something when she thought about the expression on her father's face when she'd told him that she and Brent were going to get married.

There was a time when even she had thought they wouldn't make it. Brent was still drinking. He'd done his time. *That* was something; married in May and, with the swell of Geoffrey showing in all but her fullest dresses, a jail-widow in September. And he'd got that first start with AA when he was away. But then after the baby was born he'd started drinking again and it was worse than it had been before. Ever-Clear. That's what he called it. Pure grain alcohol. He made it himself, made his own still and everything. "You could use this for gasoline," he said, but he drank it.

He made a batch for Christmas 1972, their first as husband and wife. When they went down to her parents' cottage he'd decided it would be a good idea for his in-laws to join him in what he called a "piss-up," and he'd topped up her dad's liquor supply with his Ever-Clear. But then he drank so much of it himself he could hardly stand. He and Brian had a fight, and she told him that was it. She'd just stay with her parents – they'd offered to take the baby anyway, if she hadn't wanted to get married – and he could go to the house on Nicholson Road and drink himself to death if he wanted. She wasn't having any more. New Year's he'd quit. He'd promised her he'd stop drinking and he'd never had another one. No more Ever-Clear, no more beer and no more fights – except with her, maybe, but those weren't real fights. That was one thing about Brent. When he got mad he didn't let it build up inside him; he let you know. But they could always make up. Sometimes making-up made it better than before.

Sunday, May 13/79
2:30 P.M.

Cindy, we have just decided not to be heartbroken any more with the lack of planes in the air. Our main objective now is to

99

build up our strength so that when the snow melts we can walk out of here. I had a real bad time this afternoon. I thought for sure I was ready to die. My chest hurt, my heartbeat was like a machine gun and my breathing was just as fast. I [lay] down and prayed to God to let me know whether to fight or prepare myself for death. Like a miracle, strength returned to my arms and shoulders and I sat up and told Donna that I had to walk all the way home. I was going to.

We are eating pieces of your father to keep alive. We talked it over and decided that we knew he froze to death that first night when he gave his coat to Donna so that it would be stupid to turn around and starve to death on him. We have to make the plane ready for the night now. I love you and Geoff and Jay so much. Between you 3 and God I have been able to stay alive a week now.

The handwriting – printing, really – was laborious. In the warmth of the sun, Brent managed the ball-point pen easily. But there were not many pages left in the sheaf of paper he was using. He had burned most of the pages. Now he was hunched over the rest of them, which were bound like a notebook, and as he started his diary, he tried to ration the space.

The notebook was for Donna's school work, an assignment for Office Practice. She'd promised Mr. Hackney she'd catch up on her homework, even though she was doing well. At exam time she had stood in the top ten of the 200 kids who took Office Practice. Each page was the size of a file card, and you were supposed to mark them for filing. There was a typewritten letter on each sheet of paper, reduced from its original size, and you had to figure out whether that letter should be filed alphabetically, or by the company it came from, or by geography or – what was it Mr. Hackney said? – subjectly. You figured it out and then you marked the card with a code.

When Brent finished writing a sentence in his diary he'd read it to Donna and ask her if it was right. That made her feel better too. It was as if both of them were talking to Cindy.

It's 4 now. We just took some chairs out of the plane to see if it would give us more room to sleep. I found my watch [buried] in the snow under a chair. I had to fix the band and reset it, but I think it will work. This has been the first day that I have really had enough strength to do anything. My heart feels so good when I think of you and the kids. ... Donna and I talk continuously about how much we love you and the kids. If it [hadn't] been for her arm around me there would have been some awful close calls with depression. Death. I don't think that either of us could get out of here without the other one. There is not much to say about the first few days because all we could do is cry – eat a little and when we ran out of gas for the fire we thought we were dead for we have been without a fire for 3 days now, so you can imagine how close I want to snuggle when I get home. We always keep wondering if you people have given up hope on us. But we always come right back with a lot of negative answers. We have to go in now because it is getting cold out here. Donna and I love you all so don't give up hope because we aren't. See you tomorrow.

For a day now, they had been eating the meat regularly, but they weren't used to it. They could never get used to it. No matter how much they called it "meat" or "breakfast" or whatever, they still knew what it was. They didn't talk about it, but they knew.

It was Don, parts of Donna's father, his flesh, the flesh from which she'd sprung. They prayed every time, offering grace. "Thank thee Lord for what we are about to receive," they would say, "in the name of Jesus Christ. Amen." And then they would bite into the flesh, and when they talked after that, it was often of Don. Again and again they would remind each other of his last act, of his will that they should live.

They devised a way to prepare it. From inside the engine cowling of the plane Brent had taken a flat piece of metal called the flight lock. REMOVE BEFORE STARTING ENGINE, it read. They called it their spatula. They would spread strips of the meat on it and pound them flat with their hands, and then leave them to dry in the sun. "It's like beef jerky," Brent said. The pounding and the sun took the moisture from the meat, and they cut off small pieces with the tiny knife to eat it.

Even with the loose teeth removed, Brent had difficulty chewing the dried meat. When he had trouble getting it down, Donna would put some in her own mouth first, and soften it and then wordlessly pass it to him. They ate some each morning, just after they got up, and then a little more in the middle of the day, and some in the evening before they settled in for the night. It didn't satisfy their hunger. Their bellies still ached, and cried for more food. But it was something. The prayers helped.

Monday, May 14
9:15 A.M.

I imagine you and the kids are scrabbling about getting ready for school. Have faith because I am feeling stronger again today. My left arm is not near as sore as previous. My legs are not near as shaky. And I have managed to pull 4 loose teeth out of my bottom jaw so it feels better. The cuts on my mouth and chin are healing well. No infection. It's another beautiful day here today. The snow is melting right on schedule so within a week or so maybe we can start our walk out of here. We found your dad's camera in the snow. Donna says to make sure that ... you ... know that there has only been two things that have kept us alive. One is love and complete trust in God & 2 the love for you Cindy, Geoff, Jay, Brian, Tara, Grandma Johnson, Great Grandpa and Grandma, Ron, my mom and dad, Aunt Sue and everyone we know. When we get back we are going to have all of the relatives over to our place for a barbecue. We'll all pitch in and Donna and I want to talk to all of them about the real experience we had with God while we were out here. It is 12 noon. We are sitting in the snow and are sweating. It makes it hard on a person when no planes fly over and all you can do is keep eating and prepare for your walk out. Donna and I pray out loud all the time for the things we have received. It's funny though. No matter how hard you try there is always some point in the day you feel low. So you have to talk about them. I'm back at 2:30. 80 degrees with the reflections off the hills. We have our first BM's since we hit so we feel a lot better. Just in case but I doubt it: If I don't make it home ever again (which I will) I want you to take whatever that is mine and divide it up. I think my guns and reloading supplies should go to Geoffrey. Out of any insurance money coming put enough away in each boy's bank account for their future. Cindy, my love for you is greater than any injury or crash and that's [why] I'll probably be reading this to you in person. Just in case here is my signature. (Brent Dyer) I am still going to deliver this in person if it takes until July when the snow is all gone. ... I love you and the kids more than anything in the world. A few clouds are forming so maybe we'll get a break from the heat. There is still too much snow to walk out yet and Donna and I are both too weak. It will probably be 5 or six more days before us or the snow are ready. We are not sure [which] way to go ....

One of the few things in his mind and heart that Brent did not communicate to Cindy – and throughout his writings he maintained the style of a letter writer, or even, as in the frequent "see you tomorrows," a telephone communicant – was his growing appreciation of Donna. Or, more accurately, of what was happening to Donna. The person he had regarded as a kid sister, a girl, was becoming a woman. His love for her – and now he understood that it was love – was not sexual. In the pain and discomfort of their life on the mountain, all appetite for pleasure of any kind gave way to the need to survive. But the deep changes in her bearing now affected him. There was a nobility to her, and the aura of a growing strength of spirit that he could not have imagined under the blonde curls of someone whose chief accomplishment so far as he knew, had been to twirl a baton.

One striking example was Donna's attitude toward the consumption of the flesh. Each "meal" remained spiritual agony for her, but having faced the necessity of the act, and having felt – or, equally important, having come to believe she was feeling – some resurgence in her body, and some blunting of the cutting edge of hunger, she became grimly practical about what they were doing.

"We're going to have to eat it raw," she said one day.

"Oh, Jesus."

"We just should. Look, we're eating it anyway, and when we dry it in the sun we probably lose some of the protein. That's what we're trying to get. We're just going to have to."

They began to eat pieces of the flesh uncooked.

But there was more. From the beginning, they had leaned on each other. In Brent's darkest moments he had been able to turn to her for support: the two-cylinder engine. Her strength had been the strength of a child – almost as if her mind had been unable to comprehend the desperation of their real situation – and when he turned to her it was a momentary relief from his own fatalistic sense of realism. Now, though, she was his equal. Her ability to move around had returned before his; and as in the clearing of the snow from the plane's wings, she had been able to accomplish chores that he could not. The mobility had given her both power and pride, and they were an adult's emotions, not a child's. Now, as they reached the middle of their second week alone and faced the hopelessness of ever being helped from outside, she understood their plight as well as he. Her naïveté, such as it had been, was gone. She was his partner. And he needed her as much as she needed him.

This was not an easy discovery for Brent to accept. The world in which they'd both been raised was a man's world. Men rule their roosts on the Canadian prairie, a part of the world untouched, except in its few large cities, by many of the social forces that changed urban North America in the 1970's. Men give the orders on the prairies. Men hunt, men fish, men work the fields and make the decisions in the office. Women do the books. Women can join in some things: there are mixed curling bonspiels in the long winters, but it is the men's championships that count. Men wear peaked caps with the names of farm equipment dealers on their foreheads; women wear bouffant hairdos. On their hockey jackets, the common uniform of fall and winter, men sport crests that glorify their boyhood dreams. When women are allowed to wear hockey jackets at all, their crests declare them as a "booster," or "supporter." But on the mountainside, Brent and Donna were comrades, and Brent came to realize that nothing about their equality diminished him at all.

Constantly, Donna wanted to cry for her father. She would talk as calmly about her need to let loose totally as she did about her physical requirements. Once she told Brent that she could hold in the tears no longer, and together they planned her release. "Just cry it out," Brent said. "Let go, and I'll hold on." And she had allowed her grief to roll over her like a warm wave. But when it was over, she was together again; the catharsis had worked. She thanked Brent for his support, as formally as, on another occasion and in another place, she might have thanked him for lending her his comb. But when Brent needed to cry, she was the spirit of strength, a seventeen-year-old earth mother who could help him release his tears and not feel less of a man for doing it, and offer him a wisdom beyond her years, who could comprehend that on the other side of his brazen and impudent nature was a frightened soul, and that his tears came from the same part of his complex nature as the jokes that sometimes cheered them up.

And the tears did come. He could not have imagined himself crying before. Oh, there had been moments of remorse – that awful Christmas when he'd drunk for the last time, and he had cried as he pleaded with Cindy for another chance. And tears of self-pity – alone in the jail at Regina, thinking of what he'd done to himself. But they had been something outside himself, symptoms of emotions that, to tell the truth, he sometimes did not wholly feel. Now the emotions were overwhelming him, the horror of their situation, and the joy, the sheer, sweet joy that would come welling up inside him until it burst. The tears were not from, but *of* him, and he felt no shame.

To Donna, to this emerging woman, he could open parts of himself that even to Cindy, his beloved Cindy, he had kept closed. He could talk to her of his love for his father, and wonder why he had never bothered to tell Jimmy that he loved him. He could say that right now, at this moment, he would like to cry in his father's arms. And when he said such things he could look at his sister-in-law and know that she understood. Love? Yes, it was love – a love of life, a commitment to survival, a deep feeling in his innermost being that this unspeakable experience he was going through, this terrible, gruesome, painful, wretched ordeal was forcing him to discover himself in new ways, to feel life and all that life meant to him more deeply than he had ever felt it before.

It was, he decided, just a son of a bitch of a good thing to have happened.

The search was winding down. The Wyoming patrol, never really convinced that GYVP would have strayed far enough south to cross its borders, had packed up its operation on Saturday. Idaho, with most of the possibilities now covered, stopped flying grids not long after. In Bozeman, Sam Griggs held on, but there were no new clues to follow up.

There had been a flicker of hope over the weekend. In an unprecedented move – perhaps a comment on the presence of active politicians in the search, although no one wanted to say so – a Canadian Armed Forces Transport and Rescue squadron, invited formally by the officers of Scott Air Force Base to cross the border, sent down a Twin Otter and crew. The Otter was specially equipped for reconnaissance, with double observation windows and highly trained personnel. The Canadian plane searched all through Saturday night, and their reports of three separate fires in the mountains raised expectations. Griggs despatched ground parties to check out all three sightings, but their reports quickly dampened everyone's spirits again: the fires belonged to groups of campers and some young people in a secluded house who appeared to be merrier than the searchers would have expected on a cold weekend, and who wanted no truck with anyone representing authority.

By Sunday, more than 18,000 square miles of the map between Livingston and the heart of the Idaho mountains had been coloured in on the mapped grids, many of the rectangles several times.

One by one the volunteers began to go home, back to their jobs and families and to tell the dispirited citizens of Estevan there was no news.

Each night, as those remaining gathered in the Black Lantern Lounge of the Holiday Inn in Bozeman, the talk turned to Norm Pischke. With all their physical clues exhausted, the searchers tried more and more frequently to put themselves into the pilot's mind.

Was there something – anything – about Norm's history that would tell them where he might have gone? The talk would range on till closing time, and as the weary searchers took one last paper cup of beer to go, it would carry on in their rooms at the Holiday or Ramada Inns, or among those who had moved in to the smaller Thrifty Scot to offer support for Sharon.

A bush pilot. That was the central fact of Norm's character they would return to again and again. And, like all bush pilots, fiercely proud of his skills. Griggs had heard of these men, many of them legends of aviation history, who'd helped to open much of the Canadian frontier, flying on baling wire and moose glue, going into the teeth of sixty-mile-an-hour winds in temperatures of thirty and forty below, helping the law track maddened killers, bringing out the victims of dreadful accidents and sudden illness. When they were lucky, these men lived to write stirring memoirs and enthrall their grandchildren; when the breaks went against them, they were not heard of again. Even in the Canadian arctic, there were no old unlucky bush pilots.

As a young man, Norm had been one of them. Long before he'd settled down with Sharon he'd had his share of mercy missions and emergency landings, and he'd loved the thrill of his adventures. He'd often talked of them to his friends. Like the time he'd been taking a load of truck-springs into northern Manitoba when the weather closed in on him totally – "visibility zer-goddamn-oh" – and he'd gone down into the fog and the snow and come out just above the trees and there was a clearing, like he'd designed it, and he simply touched her down in there, using the wheels as skis.

It had seemed recently to some of Norm's friends that he missed those days and that in his career as an agricultural pilot – an ag pilot, a flatland man – he'd sometimes tried to seek out thrills. There were marks on the top of the Norm Air truck, someone said. Norm used to buzz it when he was crop spraying to see how close he could come. He'd been known to touch the odd telephone wire, too, and just a few weeks before the Boise flight he'd taken off from Winnipeg in weather so severe the highways were closed. He'd been to a seminar on flying; every other pilot there had been content to stay an extra night, but not Norm. He'd taken off and landed back in Estevan in two feet of heavy snow. Busted a wing, too, which he'd later had to have fixed, but he was all right. So was the pregnant woman who'd been his passenger.

Norm had seemed troubled in recent weeks. His business hadn't been in good shape. A lot of people in Estevan knew that. He'd been behind in his payments to Shell Oil, and there'd been some question about the accuracy of the meters on the pumps Shell was filling for him, and from which he sold fuel. The pumps had been locked, one of the Estevan pilots recalled, but Norm had taken the seals off, and someone had actually come and taken the hoses away. Even that hadn't stopped Norm. He'd pumped the fuel from the underground tanks into his spray truck, and continued to serve his customers. But that had been straightened out.

So had the business with Sharon. They'd had some bad times, sure. What pilot didn't have trouble with his wife? It was part of the job. Long trips, coming home washed out. And Norm and Sharon had even split up for a while. She'd taken their older boy, Lee, down east to some kind of Mormon group – always looking into different kinds of religion, that Sharon – and Norm had been pretty despondent when she was away. He missed her – no one could remember Norm ever fooling around – and he missed Lee. He was crazy about his kids. Would any of these troubles have bothered Norm's flying? Never, said the people who knew him. When he was in a plane, he was all pilot, among the best any of them had ever seen.

"He might have been the greatest bush pilot in the history of the world," someone said at the bar. "But if he took that Cessna into some of the country we've been flying over, he was also a goddamn fool."

Chapter Nine

Tuesday, [May] 15
7:45 A.M.

Cindy, the Lord has given us another just beautiful day again today. The birds are singing. The sun is shining and I feel great. I am getting stronger and I hope to be home in time for our anniversary on the Sat. 27 or have at least contacted you by then. My love for you has grown to such strength that there is no way to put words to it any more. It is a feeling of warmth, strength and fearfulness that fills up inside of me. . . . I sure hope the kids don't pick on Geoff while I'm gone because I know there will always be someone telling him that I'm dead while I'm far from it, so don't you worry cause all I have to do is just get a little strength back and wait for a little more snow to melt before we walk out of here. I'm going to cut some meat now for breakfast. It's 10 now. Donna has an awful swollen foot and has lost the feeling in three toes. She is massaging her foot in the sun. I just had a talk with God, and asked Him to give me courage in the approaching days. My legs are strengthening steady and I hope to walk to the top of the hill soon to pick the best direction to go. We have been drying flat thin pieces of your dad in the sun to use for food on the way out. It would sure be a lot simpler if a plane would see us. The only reason Donna and I are still alive is because of yours and God's love keeping us going. How is Dad taking it all? Tell him that I'll be okay and make him believe you. We have got to spend a lot more time loving one another when I get back. I want to make you the happiest person I possibly can. When I get there I should be able to lay that carpet.

... Donna is starting to miss her dad so I tell her that she has to keep her strength up to help her mom. She wants to take over where your dad left off with KFC stores. She could probably handle a couple of them given a little experience .... Please be strong while I'm gone because I'll be able to be strong for us when I get back. I was lucky to get out of the crash alive and it was only God who saved me from bleeding to death. ... If only we weren't so weak we could start out earlier. But we will have to trust God to keep you people safe which I know He will.

They had been ten days on the mountain now, and their days had fallen into a pattern. The routine began well before dawn, when they would awake from their troubled sleep, cold and stiff, and wait, together, to see what the light would bring. This was the worst time. Brent, checking the luminous dial on his watch, would give intermittent announcements of the crawling time, and sometimes they would play games to see how long they could go without consulting his watch. They would wait for what they guessed to be half an hour, and then one of them would say, "*Now*, it must be five-thirty," or six, or whatever, but it almost never would be.

The sun rose at seven. First, its cold rays would illuminate the wall of mountain that reached up from the plane's nose, and then it would appear from behind the tail, its warmth creeping up the hillside Norm had walked down. They were quite certain now that they would not see Norm again, and they didn't talk about him.

When the sun's rays hit the white paint of the wings above their heads, they would start to move. First Donna. She would crawl through one of the doors and reach out to test the feeling of her toes – there was still none – and the hardness of the snow's surface.

The snow was melting. The sun was warm now, as if the spring they had sensed coming to the prairies had reached down to find them on the mountainside. Donna could feel it as she made her morning excursion to the outside, and she could measure the receding of the snow by its level on the plane's fuselage. At first she was able to make her way on top of the snowbanks and slide onto the tail assembly, but by the middle of their second week, she had to climb to the tail, and pull herself onto its surface. She would sit with her knees drawn up to her chin, rubbing her numb feet and imagining herself back at the family cottage with no cares on her mind. She would drift into a mindless reverie. She could feel the sun baking through her clothes, and as the day moved toward noon she would begin to remove the outer layers.

Brent, too, was able now to move from the plane; further effort was beyond him. By noon the sun was almost uncomfortably hot, and they would let themselves soak up the warmth; when sweat ran down their foreheads they would brush it off with a finger and lick the salty moisture.

There were occasional and frightening turns in the weather. On the second Tuesday, just before dark, a sudden wind blew over the canyon and came rushing down on the plane, as powerful and terrifying as the storm that had helped to blow the Cessna out of the sky. First, the sky grew quickly dark. A gust blew a piece of carpeting out of the windshield. Snow started to ride in the currents. Brent was too weak to move. Donna climbed up on the nose of the plane and tried to stuff the carpeting back in the gaping windshield. She could see the mountaintops around them disappear into the darkening cloud. The wind snarled and whistled, and the plane shook, and they had visions of it being torn from its icy moorings and hurled down through the boulders and the trees below. They huddled together inside, afraid to leave for fear that the wind would sweep up the plane like Dorothy's house in *The Wizard of Oz* and leave them there without shelter. There was nothing they could do. They waited in the plane and prayed. The wind stopped as suddenly as it had begun. In half an hour, the sky was clear again. They were sure it was a sign from God. In the silence of the wind's wake, they thanked Him.

Their physical condition continued to improve. Brent regained some use of his left arm, which hung from the damaged shoulder. His legs were losing their shaky feeling. Donna's wrist still ached but she was able to use her hand. As disabling as the pain now was their weakness. They couldn't *do* anything.

From time to time they would see small animals – squirrels mostly, but once a rabbit – moving furtively through the snow. Brent removed a wire from the Cessna's engine and fashioned a snare. It was hopeless. He was too clumsy to move to where they'd seen the animals. None of the dead vegetation was springy enough for him to fashion a trap. He thought about making a slingshot, but there was no elastic. He considered Donna's bra! That would be one for Smokey the Bear, he said. Hi kids, I'm Smokey and I have a tip for you if you're lost in the woods with your girlfriend .... No, he couldn't.

Steadily they worked on improving the quality of their life inside the cabin. They cleaned up as much as they could of the debris from the crash, picking out the largest sheets of glass to shove back into the front windshield. By arranging pieces of the carpet, like wild birds scavenging for material for a nest, they managed to make the cabin almost airtight, and when the sun fell in the early evenings, they crawled back inside to begin the endless wait through the night. Each evening, though, they enumerated whatever blessings they could find in the day that had just passed: the good weather, the ability to write the diary, the return of what, compared to their condition the week before, now seemed to them like health.

Thursday, [May] 17
8:30 A.M.

I walked to the top of the mountain this morning and have picked a path which we are going to walk out on. It couldn't be a better morning. No winds. The sun is shining. Birds are singing. God has done it again. I've decided to sell my old truck & give up working on it and set hunting aside for this year so that during the summer I can spend more time & take the kids to Regina in the fall. Donna says that her mom will let us use the trailer & van for the holiday I have planned for the end of June. We would 1st of all take off to Waskesiu up by P.A. Spend a couple of days there, then we would move west to Banff where we could use about 2–3 days in that area shopping at Calgary & Edmonton, Red Deer etc. When we get tired of that we'll move down thru Osoyoos & the Okanagan Valleys & Harrison Hot Springs & have fresh fruit salad and soak up some sun in the mountain parks. From there we could go out to Vancouver, where we would pick Donna and your mom up & spend time with more shopping in Vancouver & Victoria. We could see Bouchart Gardens & Enchanted House and all of those things. Your mom can visit with relatives there. ... On our way back we'll take the opposite route we came in on. ... Back through Fort McMurray and that whole route that you & I ran away on. I have been getting such bad heartburn the last few days that I lit a fire over some trees close by and cooked everything before I ate it. I hope it is going to help because I had to sleep sitting up all last night. I am going to lay down now for a few minutes so I will see you later.

Brent's casual reference to lighting a fire – almost an afterthought in a day whose highlight had been the walk to the top of the mountain – gave no indication of the exultation they had felt when they first saw its flames. They had been without fire for a week. There had been no fuel. Now, on their second Thursday, they had accomplished two chores. Brent had been able to pick up enough twigs and sticks to make a small pile outside the plane. And Donna, working away with the coat hanger, had induced enough gasoline from under the wing to soak a rag. Laying the rag on their kindling, Brent flicked his Bic lighter ... and flicked it and flicked it, until a tiny spark seemed to catch the rag, and then he had blown with all the breath he could push through his aching mouth until it burst into light. Through the day they had fed the fire with all the wood that was small enough to move.

Brent's spare prose belied the agony of his walk up the mountain too. From the nose of the dead plane to the summit of the hill into which they had crashed was no more than 200 feet, rising at an angle of forty-five degrees. It had taken him an hour and a half to make the journey, scrambling, crawling, moving through the snow on his knees. Every few minutes he had to stop to catch his breath and rest his muscles. All the way up, he was unable to keep himself from imagining what he might see on the other side: a town, the smoke of furnaces, perhaps the glitter of a restaurant. Or a highway? With cars and trucks zooming back and forth on the routine errands of civilization. He could just roll down there and raise his arm for help, and they would come to get him, and warm him and feed him. No, he'd tell them, he could wait to eat. They had to go back and get his sister-in-law, who was alive too, who had survived these twelve days only by her own courage and her faith in God. Yes, he would wait for her, and while he was waiting he would place a call to Cindy. How casual he would be! "Hello there. Sorry I couldn't call earlier, but there was no phone where we were. Donna? Sure, Donna's all right. They've just gone to get her in a nice warm helicopter." And *then* he would eat. Let's see now, what would he have first? Maybe just a glass of milk. Good cold milk, with little bubbles on the top of the glass. Yes, that's what he'd have first, just savouring it and impressing everyone with how calm he was. Will you *look* at that? Nearly two weeks he's been without food and he's so *calm*. Let's give him a nice bed, with flannel sheets and a thick warm comforter. When we get the girl back here they can eat together. His wife says she'll be right here. She's chartered a jet. Now, all he had to do was move his leg a little higher, and get hold of that little Christmas tree with his good arm and he could heave himself up to ....

The summit was both exhilarating and heart-breaking. To the west he could see what looked like a distant meadow, flat and green amid the grey and white of the mountains. The rest was wilderness. No town, no highway, no buildings. No sign even that man had ever reached this land. But this *had* to be the way out. Not down the valley, where Norm had gone, but out from here, along the ridge he was standing on now, and then down and into the forest that started below. Something told him this was the way. He knew it. Kneeling, he asked God for a sign, but all he could feel was the certainty they'd make it. The certainty came over him with a tingly feeling. He could feel it move through his legs and up into his mind. That was it – the sign. To the west he saw clouds hanging over small V-shaped gaps in the mountains, and as he stared at them he knew, just *knew*, that they were put there for some reason, like a huge supernatural traffic beacon. That would be their route. He had got up here once and he could do it again. They would walk toward the clouds.

Friday [May] 18/79
1 P.M.

I feel real good. We both are in real good spirits. I am going to
try to call you for our anniversary or, better, be home. Cindy,
you are going to notice me a changed person to the better when I
get home. I want to spend time with my family. Always, listen to
the kids. Read them [stories], play games with them in the yard,
read them to sleep at night. You & me & them are going to get
up in the mornings and have breakfast. I'll pick Geoff up at
noon. I want to learn how to cook. I'm even going to help you
with the dishes. My heart is so full of joy to do all the simple
things I have always missed. We've gotta get Geoff's pool up &
try out that new boat, we have got to have every last relative &
friend from town over to a big barbecue & everyone has to bring
a small something that they made themselves. I have found God
in my heart, Cindy, & He is here to stay. I'm going to talk to our
preacher when we get back & also your priest and between the 2
I'm going to pick a church & we are going to go as many Sun-
days as possible and there will have to be a good reason why not.
Maybe you were right when you said a person can find God at
any time. He kept me alive while all the blood ran out my neck. I
think I had given myself up as dead, but no, He has turned me
around, made me feel better, put fight back in my limbs, He has
me on the road to recovery, then I get upset because it takes a
while. He then gives me hope & inner peace so that I may stay
until I am strong. He took the clouds full of snow away from the
mountains and now is bathing them in sunshine. This is the
same God who was able to stop me from drinking. This person I
now choose to lead my life for me and I will follow to the best of
my understanding. My family & I shall reap the benefits. You
don't know how I can hardly wait to sleep with Geoff in the tent
this summer. We'll get a new one & we'll all sleep out there. I
want to be able to get up at 7:00 in the morning, go out to the
patio and have a nice breakfast for the 4 of us. If it's too cold, 1st
thing, I'll go down to work then & come home when you people
are ready even it is 9 or 10 o'clock. We are just going to have the
greatest life together from now on. I have a fantastic idea for a

roast. I want to try to barbecue. I want to take a piece of ham (round 3–4″) boneless about a foot long. This piece you inject a real & strong orange sauce. And cook it till it's just about done. Around the outer edge put a glaze sauce & add here crushed pineapple. Next you'll need a piece of boneless 1½″ thick steak to wrap the ham. Again you wipe the outside of the steak with pineapple sauce. You now tie it all up in a round log. (*Note* pre-cook steak in boiling sauce.) Insert onto your spit with toothpicks you hold half cherries to the outside of the log. A sauce for the outside glaze could be made of orange, cherry and pineapple, much like [Shirley] Temple. With use of meat ther-mometer you can tell when inside is really warm. Just put on spit and let cook. Side dishes should include *fresh* pineapple & fruits. Tall glasses of fruity drinks with green leaves at top. Corn on the cob with main meal. Small serving fresh salad. Long French bread & bread sticks. For dessert: strawberry shortcake & for the kids popsicles made in layers of pineapple, orange, cherry and lime flavours. Donna said that she would get us a case of hamburgers from one of the stores if at all possible. She hasn't figured out how to write it off. We are getting a little cold now because it is six here. We are going to have to go to bed now until about 7 or 8 in the morning when it is warm enough to go back outside. Neither of us sleep much & my heartburn is always bad. See you in the morning.

On Friday the whiskey-jack came. About the size of a pigeon, with a black head and a grey body, it first perched on the thin branch of the tree the plane had struck and just sat staring at them. It flew to another tree, then hopped to the ground. Donna called to it. Back to a branch it flew, unafraid. Brent looked for a rock small enough to throw.

"Don't."

"I can get it. It's big enough to eat."

"Just don't."

"You don't want it?"

"It's some kind of sign. Look. It's trying to tell us something."

"I'd rather eat it."

"Maybe it knows the way out of here."

"Don't be stupid. It's a *bird*."

"Maybe it's a sign."

"A guide?"

"Just a ... I don't know. Something live to follow."

"Come on, Donna."

"I really think it's come to tell us something."

"We'll see."

Brent stopped looking for a rock.

Chapter Ten

By vocation, Dick Hatfield is a guidance counsellor in the high school at Laurel, Montana, some one hundred miles north of Livingston, but by avocation he is a man of what he calls "a hundred different things." He is a mountain man. He is interested in survival, and he gives courses that teach, among other things, how to start a fire with a piece of ice (you shape it with the warmth of your hands into a magnifying lens). He carves belt buckles out of elk horn, and sometimes when he runs out of antler material he consults his friend Clyde Praye. A distinguished-looking sixty-five-year-old, Praye, who looks a bit like Arthur Fiedler in small-town clothes, makes most of *his* living by the practice of reflexology, the comforting and treatment of bodily disorders by manipulation of the feet. Clyde Praye is also a dowser. To most people outside the field, dowsers are people who use forked sticks to find water. To its practitioners and their followers, dowsing is much more sophisticated and useful. It can be applied to everything from metallurgy to medicine.

Clyde is married to the widow of one of America's pre-eminent dowsers, and he himself, by allowing the forces of nature to move various instruments in his hands, has been able to perform a number of remarkable feats; he has diagnosed pregnancy, predicted birthdays and found missing objects by hanging his favourite device, a pendulum suspended from a string, over maps. That's how he could tell Dick Hatfield where to look for elk antlers.

Hatfield had been in the mountains on May 5, the Saturday the Cessna had gone missing, and he had been in the area near Livingston where, he read in the newspapers, the plane was last reported.

Hatfield had seen or heard nothing. He was curious. Airplanes interested him; he would have noticed the presence of one in the area where he'd been. Perhaps it was somewhere else.

He called Clyde. "Can you locate people?" he asked.

"I can only try."

Hatfield got some maps of the area around Livingston and dropped them off at Praye's house. The next day Clyde called back. "There's something in Lost Trail Pass," he said. "I think there are two people alive." Lost Trail Pass is just inside Idaho, near the Montana border, but some distance from where the search had been concentrated.

Hatfield called Sam Griggs, whom he'd met while he was teaching survival to Montana pilots.

"It's worth a try," Griggs said.

Psychics – or people who claim in one way or another to have extra-sensory powers – are a factor in nearly every search and rescue operation. Sometimes they appear to be unwitting volunteers. In November 1976, Captain Casey Pettman of the Canadian Search and Rescue office in Comox, British Columbia, received an anonymous call from someone who said he was a clairvoyant, and that he'd dreamed of a lake, the shape of which he was able to describe. Pettman was in the first stages of a search for a Cessna 182 that had been reported missing an hour before the phone call. The man was not a relative of the missing persons, nor did he know them. He'd just had an impression, he said. The lake he'd described turned out to fit the shape of Stave Lake, near Golden Ears Provincial Park, east of Vancouver. Pettman radioed a search plane. The 182 was at Stave Lake; all aboard were dead. Every SAR veteran knows similar tales.

On other SAR operations, the psychics are called in – usually by desperate families, as the relatives of the Uruguayan football players reached across the seas for assistance (without success, as it turned out) from the Dutch clairvoyant Gerard Croiset in 1972.

Mostly, however, the clairvoyants just emerge. They come forward like a ghostly reserve battalion, ready to offer assistance. They have been known to get in touch with North American SAR offices from as far away as Sweden and India. Curiously, to those who doubt their sincerity, they virtually never seek personal reward. They are just people who have been moved by dreams or visions or other parapsychological experiences, and to whom those experiences are as real, and as potentially helpful, as those of people who report sightings of the plane or other physical clues. The clairvoyants present a dilemma to the SAR professionals, who tend to be sceptics, but who are faced with the possibility, which is never diminished by past failures, that the psychics may have real information. No search master would like to be known as the person who dismissed a suggestion from a clairvoyant only to find later that the psychic information was correct, and that by following it up he would have found his quarry. As a result, suggestions that come from supernatural sources are fed into the same store of information as those that come from anywhere else, and they are checked out.

The search for GYVP was no exception. The logs in Boise and Bozeman show several approaches from the extrasensory world. A "Mother Teresa" – she gave no other identification – called Worthie Rauscher with some hints. A man wrote from Portland, Oregon. A woman in Estevan sent in, via Sharon Pischke, some notes she had written down when her "hand was guided by God." In the scraggly handwriting, the searchers were able to make out what they took to be the words "Ball Mountain." And in spite of the fact that there are dozens of peaks throughout the cordillera called Bald or Baldy, a pilot from Idaho spent a day searching the one nearest to the centre of Rauscher's grid, with negative results.

Clyde Praye, however, seemed somehow a different case. For one thing, there was the enthusiasm of the schoolteacher Hatfield – scarcely a crackpot. For another, the site he had suggested in Lost Trail Pass turned out to be the location of an emergency landing strip on which two Montana pilots had brought a plane down unexpectedly just before the disappearance of GYVP. They hadn't reported it and were chagrined when the SAR people ran them down. For yet a third: Clyde Praye had impressed one of the most active search pilots, Bert Swainson, a helicopter man who had flown up to Laurel to ask Praye, with some cynicism, to tell him where the elk herds were that season. After consulting his maps and pendulum, Praye had told him. He was right; Swainson was impressed.

Sam Griggs, by now virtually out of other leads, called Hatfield back.

"Some of the family is still in Bozeman," he said. "Shall I tell them to get in touch?"

"Sure."

The next day Brian Johnson, who had steadfastly refused to give up, called. He was interested. Could Clyde tell them anything more?

Hatfield went back to Clyde's house. "It's back to the drawing board," he told the dowser.

Clyde went to work. He spread out large scale geological maps of the possible area. One at a time, he began to search them. Across each map he would lay a metal ruler. Over the map, carefully suspended from his hands by a four-inch ring, he hung his pendulum, a French-made device shaped like a child's top, with a non-magnetic finish and a compass embedded on its upper hemisphere. He moved the pendulum back and forth in the same pattern the SAR planes used to cover their rectangles and quadrants, hovering over each area to wait for motion in the apparatus. When it worked, the pendulum would have a life of its own, like an aerial ouiji board. Hatfield had seen it suddenly spinning of its own accord, working up enough force to act as a gyroscope, tilting until it spun horizontally. There was no way Clyde could have guided it. Now, though, there was little action. Maybe it was Hatfield's own presence. "Not there," Hatfield kept saying. "They've already looked there. No, it couldn't be there." Clyde was discouraged. In future he wouldn't let anyone in the room with him when he was working, he resolved, not even Dick.

Then, over a map of the north fork of the Salmon River, the pendulum began to twitch. "I think I have something here," Clyde said. "Tell me the name of the pilot again."

"Norm. Norm Pischke. It was a Cessna."

"I don't know," Clyde said.

"Is it worth looking?"

"I seem to sense two towers, maybe fire towers. They should be near two fire towers."

"I'll call the son."

Brian thought it was worth acting on. Nearly anything was. He said he'd get his cousin Mel Grimes, another of the hard core of Johnson relatives still in Bozeman, to take a look in the twin-engine aircraft he'd brought down from Saskatchewan. Did Hatfield know the suggested location?

"I have the map right here."

As soon as he could get away from his school duties, Hatfield drove to Bozeman. The weather was ominous. They sat around the hotel for most of the morning. In the afternoon the skies cleared. For four and a half hours, they flew and flew again over the valley of the Salmon's north fork. Nothing. Their eyes were straining.

"I'm sorry," Dick Hatfield said.

"It was worth it," said Brian. "Let me look after your expenses. Breakfast and that, your gas."

"Don't be silly," Hatfield said. "I just wanted to help. We both wanted to help. I'm just sorry we couldn't find them. I hope they're all right. That's tough country we were looking at."

Saturday [May] 19/79
9:15 A.M.

> We just finished breakfast and are sitting in the sun. It is now time to prepare to leave ourselves. Bad weather now we will know is a sign from God to hold off for a few more days. Our feet got pretty cold last night & we are now just getting back into shape. Donna could hardly walk this morning. About 12 or 1 this afternoon we are going to walk to the top of the mountain and take a last minute check of our escape route ....

In the two weeks since the crash – had it really been only two weeks? – the little plane had become their home. Now, like nomads at a change of season, they had to prepare to leave it. There was so much to do, so much to pack. On a page from Donna's Office Practice notebook – the diary – they prepared a list:

Dried meat
Bauer bag
Flight book
Flight computer
Camera
First aid kit
Belongings
Leave note
Pile stuff to be picked up in centre of floor (2 shaving kits, wallets)

Each chore seemed to lead to another. There was, for example, the matter of gas. Because they would be moving each night, they would need as much fuel from the plane as they could (a) drain from the wing and (b) carry. They had three pop bottles. Donna, the more agile at scrambling in spite of her numbed toes, climbed to the top of the left wing.

"Just jump up and down as hard as you can," Brent said.

She didn't think she could jump at all. She couldn't stand up. High up there, with the snow having melted from under the wing, she felt dizzy.

"Jump, Donna, for Christ's sake."

"Let me just stay on my knees here and I'll bounce it."

"Just get her rocking."

Her strength surprised her. She held on to the edge of the wing as tightly as she could grip, ignoring the cut in her hand, ignoring everything, just shaking the wing as if it were a teeter-totter and she was trying to throw the kid on the other end into the snow.

"It's coming. Keep rocking."

She could feel the plane wiggle beneath her.

"Keep it going. Keep it going. It's coming now. I've got one bottle full. Holy Christ, it's really pouring out of here. Keep her coming, Donna. Whoo-ee!"

The second bottle was full. The gas was running out now like water from a tap. Brent had a hard time keeping the open neck of the bottle under the shaking spigot. Too bad she hadn't been able to get up there before.

"Okay, you can stop. I got the third one full. Jeez, look at her run there."

Donna stretched out on top of the wing, worn out.

"Hey, we can get you a job when we get back. Draining planes."

"What can we use for stoppers?"

"I've got the stuff right here. Just watch this."

From their dwindling pile of firewood, he'd taken a stick of almost the right size, and broken it into three lengths. Then around each piece he wrapped a section of an airsickness bag, to fashion a cork, and around each neck he wrapped adhesive tape from the first-aid kit.

"Just like a wine bottle," he said. "Chateau Dyer, '79."

Donna clambered down from her perch on the wing. Solid ground felt good.

"There's still some gas trickling out."

"Let her run. Flood the whole goddamn hill if it wants to. Maybe she'll burn when we leave."

There was still so much to do. Quietly, and with their mood sombre, they cut their final portions of meat from Don's body, some from the thigh, and a thin strip from the back. In spite of their determination to eat as much as they were able raw and unshrunken, they decided to dry their supply for easier transport.

They were ready to take their scouting trip to the top of the hill, so Brent could show Donna where he'd planned their route.

At first, Brent had offered to go up alone, repeating his earlier journey, but Donna was not about to let him. His absence on Thursday had terrified her. She hadn't heard him leave. She'd been sitting on the tail assembly soaking up the sun and lost in thought, wondering how much she'd be able to contribute to the restaurant business when she got out. She'd have her Grade Twelve by then – if they let her graduate this spring, that is, and surely they'd let her do that, or she could write some extra exams or something – and she could help around the office, be a real part of the business, take up some of the slack from her dad's absence. Then all of a sudden she noticed Brent was gone. He'd been sitting beside her, reading over the earlier entries in his diary, and then writing some more, and now he wasn't there.

She called his name.

No answer. Oh God, where had he gone?

"Brent!"

"Up here." His voice had sounded so far away. "I'm up the hill."

"Oh, Brent, I thought you'd ... I don't know."

"I can see over the top."

"Are there any people?"

"I can see where we can walk. We can find some people."

He'd come back down then, rolling and tumbling when he couldn't stand up, and she'd felt a surge of excitement as he told her about his cloud sighting, and how he was sure the Lord wanted them to go. But the joy of discovering him at the top and of his return hadn't compensated for the fright she'd felt when he was away. Just for those few seconds, she thought he'd left her there, and she'd had a glimpse of what it would be like without him. She was determined he would not get out of her sight again.

They began to climb the hill together.

It was horrendous.

She didn't even have to look at her watch to know how long it was taking them to climb the two hundred feet to the top. She could feel the angle of the sun changing on her back. And at the summit there was ... nothing. Nothing and everything. Just mountains and snow, and more trees and boulders and hills ... they'd never get out of here.

Lying on her belly at the top of the hill they would have to climb again tomorrow – climb before they could even start on their real walk – Donna fell apart.

"We're never going to do it," she said. "We've been kidding ourselves. We're not going to see our families again. We're not going to see Cindy or Mom or your kids or Ron or Grandma and Grandpa or anybody again. We're going to die here just like Dad did. Freeze and die and no one will ever find us."

This time, Brent had nothing left to give her. The climb had worn him out. The waves of their emotions, so synchronized through much of their ordeal, with the highs of one coinciding with the lows of the other, now fell into a dreadful harmony, with sorrow reinforcing sorrow, and despondency despair. As the sun crept across the sky between the mountains, they lay on the snow of their first summit and wept.

And then Brent said, "Fuck it."

"What?"

"I said fuck it. We're getting out of here. We *can't* die. We weren't *meant* to die. God wouldn't have spared us this long if He was going to let us down now. He's just testing us."

"You mean He wants us to feel this bad."

"Everything we feel is what He wants us to feel."

"Maybe He's telling us to smarten up."

"That's right. Smarten up, you two. That's what He's saying."

"Well then, let's smarten up."

"Smarten up and get out of here."

"I don't care how long it takes me, I'm going to get out of here."

"It could be a long time."

"It could be three months, but I'm getting out. I think you're right. I think that's what He's telling us. Smarten up. You know that tingling feeling you said you had yesterday up here? I can feel it too. I've got it. We're *going*."

"We're going to be home by my anniversary."

"And my graduation."

"Right."

"Will you stand in for Dad at my graduation?"

"Sure. Goddamn right. I'll stand up there and I'll watch you get that old certificate and I'll know that's what the Lord wanted for you. And your dad too. Your dad will be there just as much as I am. He'll be looking at you and he'll say, 'That's my kid there, the one with the high marks. She was up on the mountain and she wouldn't quit.'"

"Brent?"

"Yes."

"I want to sing."

"The hymn. Shall we sing the hymn?"

"Yes. I want to thank the Lord for what He's telling us."

They began. "Holy, holy, holy ..." Through the first verse, and when they finished that, they started again, and then again, right through every time, as loud as they could, feeling as they got to "our song shall rise to Thee" that it actually *was* rising. Finally, when Brent's chest hurt too much from the exertion, they stopped, but the hymn had once again built on the joy they were already feeling, and they made their way back to the plane.

Their high spirits remained, and now, like children preparing for a holiday, they tried to clean themselves up. Donna's hairbrush, which she'd given to Brent for safe keeping, but which had fallen through a hole in his pocket and been missing inside the plane for days, had turned up during one of their tidying sessions, and now she put it to use. In the last warmth of the sun she pulled it through the tangled mass on her head. Her shoulder-length hair was one big matted knot. The brush would barely move, and when it did, as often as not, hair would come with it, great skeins of dirty blonde wool, like the stuff that comes out when you brush a dog, but more of it – handfuls of it.

"I'm going to pull it all out," she said. "I'll need a wig."

"So? We'll get you a wig. You can be a brunette if you want."

"I'm a brunette now. Look at this stuff. It's almost black."

"Matches your eyes."

"It's from the smoke."

"New way to dye hair. Sit in a Cessna 172 and burn paper. Works every time."

She kept brushing. It was all right. She couldn't get it straight, but it was better than before. They bathed their faces in melted snow, washing off as much of the accumulated dirt as they could. Brent's jaw was tender. Worse than tender. Pus was oozing from his gums where he'd pulled his teeth out. But swabbing his chin in the lukewarm water helped. In clean water, they brushed their teeth. Brent squirted shaving soap from the aerosol can, and scraped the stubble from his face. He thought of splashing some after-shave lotion on, but figured he couldn't cover the stink of his body, so left it alone. The ablutions refreshed them.

There was so much left to do. Even going through the wallets took time. They counted their cash; it became more and more like preparing for a vacation. Donna had $200 in U.S. funds set aside to pay for the dog, and another $100 – no $107 – to shop with, as well as $10 Canadian. Don had carried $160 U.S. in cash and a folder of travellers' cheques worth another $300. Brent had $61 Canadian.

"I guess you weren't going to buy much," Donna said.

"It's cheaper if you don't drink."

The total, in cash and cheques, came to $738. They made a meticulous list on one of the Office Practice sheets.

On reflection, they decided not to take the camera, but to leave it hanging on its strap. It would be the first thing any search party would notice, they figured, and inside the case they placed their note, saying they'd headed off up the mountain, and telling whoever found the camera that it belonged to Donna, and they should send it on to her. They put down her address. From the wood collected for the fire, each of them chose a sturdy walking stick.

The pile in the plane was growing higher. They'd have to leave some stuff out for the night; they could pack Don's Samsonite suitcase in the morning. The suitcase might be hard to carry. From an extension cord that led from the plane's electrical system to a now useless heater, Brent twisted an extra handle. They filled the Bauer bag. They were almost ready to go.

At six o'clock Brent wrote in the diary, keeping his report on the day's activities brief. "We were able to squeeze 3 bottles of gas from the plane to use as fire lighter," he wrote. "We cut a little extra [meat] for our journey." He didn't mention the emotional scene on the mountaintop.

"I'm going to say goodnight for now," he finished. "I don't imagine I'll talk to you until tomorrow night. Kiss the kids a sweet one for me. Go to sleep with a prayer on your lips. I'm sure our love will once more be united. Talk to you tomorrow."

They stayed outside by the fire as long as they could. It was good practice for what awaited them. They would not have the shelter of the plane on their journey, and sitting outside would give them a kind of rehearsal.

Back inside the plane, Donna kissed the cold cheek of her father's body. It would be the last night she would sleep beside it. They would have a service in the morning, before they left.

Outside, in the dark, they heard the whiskey-jack.

III
The Walk
May 19 to May 24

My DIARY + LAST will.
To my w.fe CINDY DYER
ALSO to my ChiLDREN Geoffrey
+ JAmie.

TO CINDY DYER.
⬚⬚⬚ NicholSON Rd.
ESTEVAN SASKATCHEWAN, CANADA
S4A-IT8

PLEASE
MAIL
IF FOUND PLEASE

Signed
Brian Dyer

Chapter Eleven

The sighting of the body was reported at 1:20 on Sunday afternoon by Twaink Kalikowski, a young woman who managed, in spite of her heavy down jacket and fisherman's gear, to look pretty as she lumbered into the sheriff's office in Livingston. Livingston is the capital of Park County, which runs south to the Wyoming border, along both banks of the Yellowstone River, and covers the northern end of Yellowstone Park. Twaink had been going after trout, she said, and she'd had a good view of the river from her perch, about three miles south of town, down by the Melody Inn. She'd cried out in alarm, but the two men she'd been fishing with had been too far up the bank to get down for a look. Nevertheless, she was sure. A body floating face down in the spring-swollen current, with a blue flannel shirt, or perhaps a sweater, torn to reveal a white T-shirt underneath. Male or female? She wasn't sure.

Sheriff Ben Huckins was impressed. Much of Park County had been air-searched by now, but as he had travelled through the river valley, asking questions and putting out the word about the missing Canadians, he hadn't mentioned clothing. So if the girl's observations checked out they might be on the trail of a firm clue. He didn't know the girl, but he was aware of her family in town. Good people.

Time enough to check on the clothing later. For now there was action to take. He got on the radio, and before two o'clock a network of CBers was stretched out from the Melody Inn downstream, one person every quarter mile, staring into the eddies. A jet boat was launched into the river, floating downstream on the alert. The search went till dark. No one spotted the body.

In Bozeman the next day, Brian Johnson, still weary from his flight with Dick Hatfield, but nevertheless anxious to follow any clues, saw a brief report in the Livingston *Enterprise*. He called his uncle, Keith Johnson, who was also still in Bozeman. Keith agreed to go down to Livingston. The reporter who'd written the story could tell them little; the sheriff gave them Twaink's name. She had no phone.

They drove to her apartment, where they found her receptive and friendly. Yes, she was sure of what she'd seen. She hoped it wasn't one of their family.

Brian had no list of clothing with him, but something sounded familiar. Male or female? he asked Twaink again. She couldn't tell, she repeated. The body looked big. Colour of hair? Couldn't see it. Blond? Couldn't tell.

Brian was troubled. That night, from his hotel in Livingston he placed a call to Evelyn. Taking care to sound as casual as he could, and taking pains to ask about other matters first, he asked for a review of the clothing his mother remembered. To his relief, she seemed to think he'd found another psychic; she'd already been asked to send down photographs and a sample of Don's handwriting for others. She told Brian again about his father's leather jacket, and Donna's blue kangaroo jacket. Brian had a moment of alarm, but they chatted for a while about other things and hung up with expressions of mutual encouragement.

He placed a call to Sharon, who had returned to Estevan to be with her children. Brock Perry was with her at the Norm Air office. On an extension, he answered almost simultaneously with Sharon. Although he would have liked to, there was little Brian could do to shield Sharon from the possible tragic import of his questions. Brian felt sympathy for Sharon, although, even in the time she had been in Bozeman, when they had shared the tension of the early search, they had not become close. Brian told them both what he had learned.

Sharon burst into tears and left the phone. Brock Perry explained to Brian. Under his flight jacket Norm had worn, as he almost always wore, a turtleneck. It was white.

A pair of apparitions – doppelgängers of the mountain snows – moved slowly up the hill, climbing silently and agonizingly away from the carcass of the Skyhawk. Smoke still curled toward the morning sun from their fire of the night before, burning at the foot of the larch tree that had crumpled the wing.

From a distance, Donna might well have been taken for someone on her way – or his way, for the thick layers of their makeshift costumes hid both their genders – to the beach. Her outermost garment was the ankle-length pyjama coat, with its blue hood encasing her hair. Wrapped around the hood, like a swimmer's towel, was the brown shirt her father had been wearing when he died. Underneath the pyjama coat were, in order: Brent's Mickey Mouse sweatshirt, her own leather jacket, the zippered blue kangaroo jacket and, finally, next to her skin, her white T-shirt. Only her blue corduroy slacks covered the upper part of her legs under the robe, but her feet were wrapped first in a pair of white socks and then in two airsickness bags. Over both these layers she had forced her North Star shoes. At last, the right one would go on too. The cuffs of her cords were tucked into her socks.

Brent's feet were similarly clad: his own soft suede shoes, a pair of the airsickness bags, a pair of socks pulled up over his trouser legs. He also wore five layers of trousers: his own dress pants next to the skin; the tops of Don's pyjamas, the sleeves pulled over his legs; the pyjama bottoms; a pair of his own jeans and, finally, Donna's extra pair of jeans, which he was unable to close at the waist. Over his light shirt and sweater-vest he wore his own corduroy jacket (he had cursed himself as he put it on, remembering Cindy's advice to wear his down-filled Eddie Bauer vest instead) and Don's leather jacket. Around his middle he had wrapped and buckled Don's belt. Down his neck, he had stuffed the beach robe. As mittens, each of them wore a pair of Donna's white socks.

They had bowed their heads over Don's body in formal farewell before they'd left the plane.

"We'll come back to get you," Donna had pledged.

They weren't talking now. The climbing took all their breath.

With nearly an hour gone since their nine o'clock start they were not yet at the top of the hill they had climbed yesterday to reconnoitre. They were already behind schedule.

Before they'd set out that morning, they'd established a destination for their first day's walk: the V-shaped gap in the mountains they'd been able to see from the summit, where Brent had first seen the clouds he'd taken as a sign. But between the plan and their destination, they had set a number of smaller, more attainable goals.

At first, overestimating their strength, they had resolved to move in segments of thirty paces each. They would go thirty paces and then rest, and then thirty more. They had defined a "pace": Start with the feet together. Reach forward with the left foot. Plant the left foot. Bring the right foot forward even with the left. Plant the right. That would be one pace. Thirty of them and they'd rest. But they had soon recognized that their ambitions were greater than their stamina. They were doing segments of ten now. Left, right up to the left, left. They would try to make a rhythm of it. *One*, stand with feet together, *two*, bring the left up, *three*, bring the right up, but their feet would keep breaking through the snow, and they would tumble and the burdens they were carrying would bring them to their knees. They would poke about with the walking sticks they had chosen the previous day until they found something solid, and then heave themselves upright.

Donna carried Don's Samsonite suitcase. Into it they had packed all the plane's seatcovers except the smallest, which had served as a shroud for Don's face; two pieces of the black carpeting; the wrapped electrical cord that Brent had cut from the plane's lighting system; Don's wallet; Norm's wallet and watch; Brent's flying log, his flight "computer"; extra socks (nearly all of them burned at the toes); some items of first aid – the remainder of the Stop-Bleed, two crushed aspirins, their keys, and a piece of the broken shaving mirror; two toothbrushes, Donna's precious curling iron, Brent's Christian Dior aftershave, Donna's Charlie perfume, the Bonne Bell after-tan lotion, and finally, the Blistex burn ointment.

The contents of the Bauer bag, which Brent was carrying up the hill, were almost all utilitarian: a small cardboard of needle and thread – the kind supplied by many hotels – which they'd found in Don's shaving kit; some safety pins; the rest of the first-aid equipment, including a wire splint to use on a fractured limb; the three stoppered bottles of airplane gas, the unused airsickness bags, the spatula-shaped flight lock; a flat piece of aluminum salvaged from the plane; the top of Brent's shaving cream and, packed in snow, about ten pounds of the meat.

Left foot forward. Plant. Bring up the right. Plant. Make ten of those and rest again, sit on the suitcase. Catch breath.

Sometimes the rest stops seemed to do as much harm as good, for as they rested stiffness would creep over them, and the pain would begin to gnaw at Brent's feet; Donna's remained without feeling. It was almost better to keep going. Just do another ten paces. Let's *go*. Let's move it.

They reached the crest just before eleven.

"That's got to be the hardest part," Brent said. "It'll be easier now."

"It can't be any harder."

"I wasn't sure we could make it."

"We should try to do more than ten paces at a time now."

"Should we try thirties again?"

"Twenties. Let's just rest a while, though."

"It's time for church."

"That's what they'll be doing now at home, going to church. I wonder if they're praying for us."

"It's a different time zone."

"Do you think God knows about time zones?"

"He can hear you all the time."

"He's sure been listening to us. Look at this weather. It's really beautiful up here."

"We should have a church service."

"Right up here? Yes, we should."

"We could just pray."

"And we'll sing again. We'll sing our hymn."

"Remember when we sang it here yesterday?"

"That was the worst time. I thought I was going to give up."

"I *was* going to give up."

On the hill, they conducted their brief service, praying and then singing, and then praying again, thanking the Lord for the weather and for the strength they now felt they had.

"Let's change suitcases," Brent suggested. "I'll take your dad's, and you can carry the Bauer bag. Don't drop it. It's got the gas in it."

"Don't worry. Thanks. It should be easier."

"Put the strap over your shoulder."

Down from the ridge of the mountain on which they were standing – the edge of the canyon where the Cessna had met its end – a thin ledge, a kind of finger of rock, seemed to form a natural path that would lead them toward their day's destination. They began moving down it, now frequently able to step off thirty paces before they needed rest. The ledge led down for several hundred feet, and then curved off to the right, beneath a crag. As they neared the corner they began to hear a sound that was almost, if not quite, as welcome as a human voice.

"Water," Donna said.

"I think so. Must be running down out of that crag."

They could see it as soon as they rounded the corner, a small rivulet that seemed to spring from the very forehead of the rock. They hobbled toward it. It was the first time in two weeks they could drink water without melting snow. From the Bauer bag they dug out the top from Brent's shaving soap container, and they sat in the sun, dipping the cup into the chilly stream and tilting their heads back in glee as they drank it, letting it spill down their chins and run icily over their clothes. It was worth it. Water! They'd forgotten how good it could taste, and what a luxury it was to have more than they needed.

They decided to stop for lunch, taking some of the dried meat from the Bauer bag. Then, rested, they set off again down their finger of rock toward the valley below.

From one angle, Brent, straining his eyes, thought he could see single lines of tire tracks on a hill in the distance.

"Couldn't that be something?" he asked. "Maybe they come out here to race motorcycles. Like those hill climbs, you know?"

It was an illusion. They remembered the mirages from their first days.

They pressed on.

As they drew closer to the valley floor, they realized it was not land at all, but a lake, now frozen and covered by snow, but here and there in the sunlight were puddles of what was obviously slush or even water. It would be too dangerous to cross, and too hard-going even if

136

the surface held. They started uphill again, climbing to their right. The turn, they figured, headed them north. The climb slowed them down again. Brent would try to plant the suitcase uphill, and use it as a handhold to haul himself upward, but it would sink into the snow, or begin to slide down toward him, and he would have to jam his walking stick deep into the snow to act as a brake. The Bauer bag was almost as troublesome to Donna. Sometimes their legs would sink into the snowbanks up to their thighs, and they would crawl along on their bellies, or just wriggle to find a firm spot. Fighting their way up to the top of the hill took all their energy. When they reached the crest again and found a large tree standing in greeting, they decided they would camp for the night. There were small trees around, and some bushes. It was much like the ground around the plane, and if they stopped now and rested and laid down their luggage, they could move around and gather firewood for the night.

On the farthest of his excursions for the wood, Brent reached the hill's edge, and in the lowering light thought he could see the green meadow he had noticed on Thursday, when he had first climbed to the top of their own mountain.

"See it, Donna? Over there. Just a soft green plain in the middle of those far mountains."

"Well, kind of."

"They wouldn't waste that kind of country up here, you know. There'd be farms, or a ranch or something. People. If we could just get there ..."

"It looks so far."

"Maybe we can't make it tomorrow. But we could start that way. I told you the Lord was showing us the way."

"How far did we come today."

"Not very far, I guess. It feels like twenty miles but I doubt if we made two. How are you feeling?"

"Okay. What about you? *Two* miles?"

"Well, like along the ground. We probably went twice that counting up and down. I'm okay. Let's get that fire going while there's still some light."

A cold wind was rising.

To save wood, they kept the fire small until the dark came. In the twilight, Brent wrote his daily note to Cindy:

... The walk today & most likely tomorrow will be the hardest. By the end of tomorrow we should have reached a type of valley that should take us out to some kind of civilization.

And then came yet again the thoughts of food:

Donna & I are just dying for some of your strawberry shortcake. As soon as we get back you can make us some. We both want extra large pieces. ...

Both of us were so tired when we got here we didn't think we could make it any more. But if this wind goes down we'll have an easy night and be right back at it in the morning. We have got our socks dried out and are working on our shoes. If we can reach this valley tomorrow we'll be clear of snow.... So far everything is running along real smooth & should get better as the days go. I sure miss you & the kids & can hardly wait to see you again. I get so sick to my stomach when I think of how you must be feeling. ... As soon as I get back we'll lay the carpet in the patio and use up some of those lobsters & get some good [steak], not to forget corn on the cob. If I could sell my truck we will have lots for that trip I told you about. There is quite a strong wind here which is making it quite miserable. I have got to get covered up a bit so I will see you later, love. Kiss the kids goodnight for me.

The wind kept getting worse. Their socks, as Brent had mentioned to Cindy, were hung out to dry on the extension cord which they had strung between two trees. Now they began improvising a shelter from the pieces of carpet, standing the suitcase up to make one wall, and using their extension-cord-clothes-line as a ridgepole. They tried to chink it with branches of the evergreen and even stuck the piece of aluminum they'd brought from the plane into one drafty corner, but the wind kept whistling through, blowing the heat of the fire back and forth across their bodies, and filling their eyes with smoke.

"Maybe we're lucky we've got this wind," Brent said. "That wood's pretty wet. It would go out without the draft."

"I just wish we could get out of the smoke."

Before they settled in for the night, they inspected each other's injuries. The infection in Brent's jaw was worse; it appeared to have abscessed between the gum and shattered bone. The cut on Donna's hand was healing, but the hand was badly swollen. Brent bathed it in the Stop Bleed, and put on a clean dressing from the first-aid kit. Using the small jackknife, they tried to clean their fingernails. They couldn't shake the sense of filth they'd brought with them. They stacked the fire to last the night, unmindful of the smoke. The flames cast a light around their shelter, and on the other side of the suitcase they could make out a small grey shape, fluttering.

"Will you look at that," Brent said.

"It's the bird!" said Donna. "I know it's the same one. It's the same whiskey-jack that was back at the plane. He's coming with us. He's going to get us out of this."

Sharon's tempestuous reception of the news of the reported sighting in the river was characteristic of the way she was set apart from the other women with whom she shared the void of waiting. She is a mercurial woman, a volatile spirit. Even in the briefest conversation her moods can range from giddy to sombre, from euphoria to despair. Her round, rich eyes stare straight at whomever she talks to, drinking her listener in; they can twinkle with joy and well with tears in the same sentence. She gives the impression that her soul smoulders not far beneath the surface.

In Estevan, while not alone, she was not a part of the general life of the community. Her living quarters, a former mobile home set into concrete near the Norm Air office, was lined with books that ranged from obscure religious texts to the memoirs of bush pilots, and she read constantly and voraciously.

With Norm, before they settled in their own business, she'd led a gypsy life; when he left the bush to fly crops, they'd moved from town to town like the barnstorming pilots of old, often sleeping for nights at a time in a tent by the most convenient air field. That's where they'd been living when a wandering magazine writer who'd used Norm for a charter had mentioned the availability of the Estevan business, and almost the next day, it seemed, they were winging their way down to begin negotiations.

She liked the life, although sometimes the emptiness of the landscape that reached to the horizon in all directions from the airstrip made her long for the woods of Manitoba, and sometimes she would take one or the other of her sons and disappear to a property she and Norm had bought near their hometown.

She cared passionately for her sons. And in the evenings after she had returned from Bozeman, when her eldest, Lee, a lean teenager in heavy glasses, who seemed to inherit both Norm's calm nature and Sharon's depth, rode his bicycle up and down outside on the airstrip, up and down, up and down, her heart would want to reach out through the window and embrace him. One night she heard tapping at the typewriter as she tried to sleep, and the next morning found that Lee had been trying to express his longings and his love for his father in a private poem. She didn't know how to soothe his pain. The earlier troubled time of her marriage had served only to intensify her love for Norm. She was his woman, as she had been since they were kids together in Moose Horn, when they would lie on their backs while Norm described the planes that sometimes worked their slow way across the sky. She had a hard time, an almost impossible time, keeping her need for his return to herself. She was worried and afraid.

Cindy Dyer's energy is as kinetic as Sharon's is actual. Intense, too, but in a different way. Repose does not come easily to her slim frame. After the bad first months of her teenage marriage, she had gone back to school, picking up subjects and credits with an ability that often amazed her teachers. The house on Nicholson Road is a model of interior decoration; comfortable furniture is arranged in apparently casual conversational groupings. Pictures fill the walls. Healthy plants stand in the corners. The ashtrays are always clean.

Although she knew any news would almost certainly come to her mother first, she was reluctant to leave the house. She didn't want people staring at her downtown. Poor girl, they would say. She didn't need it. She could handle it. She could keep busy at home.

Weekends were worse even than that first Tuesday when Geoff had come home from school with the news about the show and tell. During the rest of the week Cindy could pretend to herself that Brent was away at work, and even with little Jay at home there wasn't the steady reminder of Brent. She could do her housework, and friends would call, and from time to time she could lose herself in a soap opera, or, when it got really bad, take Jay over to her mother's. But on the weekends, every moment reminded her of the absent man of the house.

In nearly eight years Brent and Cindy had never been apart for a weekend – not a single one. Weekends were when they shopped together, or made plans to fix up the house, or played with the kids, or visited relatives – always as a family. While both of them had friends and interests of their own, they had become each other's best friend, as lover and spouse. And with Geoffrey around the house, a miniature of the Brent Dyer perpetual motion machine, Brent's absence was underlined. There was one thing about Geoffrey, though: whenever her own imagination teetered toward the unthinkable, Geoffrey buoyed her up. "My daddy's coming home," he would tell her, and his solemn eyes left no room for doubt.

To everyone who saw Evelyn Johnson during the time of waiting, her serenity was a subject of wonder. "I don't know how she does it," they would say to each other. "She's like Jackie Kennedy," one of her sisters remarked one day. The sisters – Joey, Marie, Kay, Veronica, all with husbands and lives of their own – flocked to her. Marie moved right in almost as soon as the plane was reported missing. But sometimes it seemed to them as if it were she offering the comfort and they who needed her strength. "It's her nurse's training," Marie said to Joey.

She had fought hard to become a nurse, leaving the family farm at Lampman to endure the severe training of the Grey Nuns. From a family that had only recently survived the Depression, an era that touched and scarred southern Saskatchewan more deeply than any other part of North America, there was no extra money. She coped. She dined on peanut butter and jelly some nights, but she got her cap, and on the night of her graduation, Don Johnson, the dashing and ambitious young bookkeeper with an automotive supply house, had given her her diamond. Even when she'd left her nursing job with the Air Ambulance she'd continued to work, helping Don with his books, becoming a part of his growing business. A handsome woman who speaks slowly and carefully, choosing her words with care, Evelyn kept her emotions hidden from her family.

It was only during the nights that she cried.

Tuesday night, May 22, was election night in Canada, and by the time the polls closed in Saskatchewan it was already evident that the man who had dominated the nation's politics for more than a decade, the easterner and French Canadian Pierre Trudeau, would almost certainly now give way to the westerner and small-town Conservative Joe Clark.

In Estevan, which had long ago made up its mind against Trudeau, another piece of news was making the rounds, and causing phones to ring: the "body" in the Yellowstone River. The story had broken in Saskatchewan on CKCK Regina, which interrupted its election coverage at 5:45 that afternoon, and carried the story all evening. Judy Gingras, a niece of the Johnsons, was the first of the family to hear it. She called her Aunt Joey, who in turn called her brother-in-law, Chuck Gheyssen, in Stouton, who, she knew, was on his way to Evelyn's. "Try to keep her from watching television," she said, "even though it probably isn't anything." Then Joey called the radio station and told the switchboard operator what she thought of a station that would run a story like that without even checking with the family.

Brock Perry heard the news in Estevan. He had seen what even the faintest hint had done to Sharon's composure the night before and his first thought now was of his friend Brent's wife, Cindy. He called.

"Hope you're not watching TV," he said.

"No," she said. "Why?"

"Oh, well, I just don't think you should watch it tonight."

By the time the news reached Estevan, however, it was no news at all. Penny Poole, the Regina *Leader-Post*'s Estevan correspondent who had gone to Bozeman as a journalist and had stayed to fly in the search planes, was now back to her regular assignments. She had been in Weyburn covering the federal election news when the office had called and told her to use the contacts she'd built up in Montana to check out the story of the body, or "bodies," as the media were now reporting.

She got Sheriff Huckins on the line.

"There *are* no goddamn bodies," he said.

"But –"

"There's nothing there." He hung up.

No confirmation, the *Leader-Post* reported.

And there never was. Whatever Twaink Kalikowski had seen – and to this day she is sure it was a human body in blue flannel with a white T-shirt underneath – it was not Norm, nor any of his passengers. After two days of scouring the Yellowstone, the searchers gave up. The story disappeared from the news.

Chapter Twelve

Monday started with foreboding. Donna couldn't walk. Literally couldn't move. She'd left her walking stick about twenty feet from their night's shelter, and when she woke up she couldn't get to it. It was there, sticking out of the snow, but it might as well have been in Estevan. It was the stiffness. Sunday's walk must have done it. She was stiff and weak at the same time, and she had to ask Brent to get the stick for her just so she could pull herself upright.

There, that was better, but she was still weak, and she didn't know how far she could walk that day.

"We should try and make that plain."

"I'll try."

"That's all you can do. Yesterday had to be the hardest. It will just get easier now."

"Yesterday I could walk."

"You didn't look like it."

"What do you mean?"

"You looked like you were trying to wiggle the whole way on your belly."

"And what do you think you looked like? A long-distance runner?"

"Yup. That's me. Brent Dyer of Estevan, Saskatchewan. He's coming into the stadium now, folks. He's finishing his last lap. He's going to make it. He's going to beat all those foreigners! Here he is! The winner! He's stepping up to get his gold medal from the king of—"

"The king of liars probably."

"Just the king. King of the world. Let's go, eh? Let's move on out of here."

They had decided to stay on the top of the ridge as long as they could. The ridge was descending now, and by trying to walk along its spine they would have an easier route into the valley, avoiding the soggy lake they could still see below them. On the ridge – the finger of the mountain, as they called it – the snow lay more thinly on the ground, but to their dismay they found the going over the rough rocks, which varied from small pebbles to boulders the size of station wagons, even harder than over the thick snow of the day before. Their ankles twisted with almost every step, and picking their way through the obstacles, they were unable to keep even the measured, tortuous pace of their first day. As hard as they tried to move in units of ten or twenty or thirty paces, they kept running into natural barriers that forced them to rest.

The finger of the mountain seemed to stretch on forever. By the time the sun hung high over their heads, causing them to sweat and struggle out of some of the outer layers of their clothes, they had covered far less ground than they had hoped. The break in the mountains that led to the plain – to see the meadow itself – was scarcely closer than when they'd set out.

Then Donna had her accident. Rather than carrying the Bauer bag as a beast of burden would, she'd taken to swinging it ahead of her, sometimes using it as an anchor to throw over a high rock ahead and then pull herself forward. Sometimes she just let it drag along the ground behind her from its strap. She came to a particularly large rock. She whirled the Bauer bag and began to swing it over, and as she did so, she saw, as if in slow motion, one of the zippers open, and from out of the pocket it had been holding closed went one of the precious bottles of gasoline. The bottle shattered against the rocks. Now there were two.

"Three gas bottles ..." Hysterically, she almost started to sing.

For once, Brent didn't try to cheer her up. This could be serious.

"Let me take them," he said.

"No, it's okay. I'll just be more careful."

"The Bauer bag was the wrong place to carry gas anyway. Let me take them. I can stick them in the pockets of your dad's jacket."

"Okay. You're not mad, are you?"

"No, I'm not mad. There're still two left."

Half an hour later they were down to one. He must have dropped the other. He wasn't sure where. Probably in one of the patches of snow that still lay along the ridge, or else he'd have heard it fall. He must have been scrambling over another rock or something, but now there was only one bottle left. He was glad he hadn't blown up at Donna.

"We'll just have to save gas from now on," he said. "We won't be able to pour it on the fire tonight. We'll have to figure out a way to soak a rag in it, or something, just like we did when we could only get a few drops out of the plane."

And finally something went right. Well, almost right. They came to a patch of vegetation that bore berries. Donna thought the bushes looked like ferns. Brent said sassafras. The plants were about the size of the astor hedge that surrounded his front yard.

"Whatever they are, do you think we should eat them?"

They had been more than two weeks now without the taste of a growing thing. Still, the berries looked sort of funny. They wished they knew what they were. Some were green, some white. The white ones scared them.

"I'm going to try a green one," Brent said. He pushed it into the gap in his mouth.

"It tastes like a pine cone. It's not bad when you get it in your mouth, but when you swallow it it's like eating a Christmas tree."

Donna took a bite.

"Piney," she said. "I don't think we should eat any more. Our stomachs must be in pretty bad shape."

"I'm not sure mine could hurt any worse. It aches all the time."

"Mine too. But that's probably just hunger. These could be poison."

"There's one here that looks like a Saskatoon. I'm going to try it."

"How is it?"

"The same. Like you could use it to caulk your canoe."

Reluctantly, they moved on. The walking grew no easier. At times it was best to crawl. They came across no waterfalls like the one they'd drunk so lustily from the day before, but here and there ripples of water murmured near the path, and they would put their mouths against the rocks and suck up as much as they could, just slurping away like thirsty hound dogs, trying to filter out the grit and the mud with their lips. Still, it was better than the melted snow.

At one o'clock, Brent stopped. Just stopped. Couldn't go any further and didn't want to. He was beat. They'd tried to go too far too fast. He had to rest.

They were down on the shoulder of the ridge now, trying to follow what seemed to be a natural path. Just below them lay a large patch of snow, big as a parking lot, only thick. It looked as though it had slid down from above all in one chunk. Brent pulled himself to a rock that stood above it, and then jumped down with the suitcase. He pulled the suitcase under him and let himself slide down to the bottom of the snowpatch. Then he crawled to some boulders in the shelter of a tree and collapsed.

Donna took command. She slid down after him.

"You sleep for a while," she said. "I'll get us settled in here."

She slogged about on her aching feet, gathering firewood. She opened the first-aid kit and used soap to wash herself and, as best she could, Brent. Remembering Brent's advice about the gasoline, she pressed one of the remaining gauze bandages across the lip of the bottle until it was wet, then, carefully covering it with twigs, used the lighter to spark it to life. With the fire going, she lay back in the sun. They could rest there for the night.

When Brent woke from the heaviness of his slumber, they ate. The meat was holding up despite the daytime heat, and not rotting as they had feared it might, although the snow they had packed it in had long since melted, and soaked through the wrapping. They resolved to use what was left of the day to gather strength; they would eat again at midnight and in the morning.

To Cindy, Brent tried to keep an optimistic front: "We just about made it to the valley between the mountains today," he lied. But then the truth started to creep through:

I ran out of strength. This side of the mountain is so rough. ...
This is the most tired I have ever been since I started writing. I
didn't think I could make the last 100 yards to our shelter, but
between Donna, God & love for you I was able to .... Cindy, I
love you & will write you later tonight by the firelight. Hug the
kids for me.

That night, his words to Cindy had a new tone. It may have been the exhaustion, or the results of his much needed afternoon sleep, which was the deepest and most restful he had enjoyed since the ordeal began. Now, just as he had been able to open himself to Donna at the crash site, he could bare his inner self to his wife. The love and the longing he had spoken about in each of the diary entries shone through every line.

The news, as always, was in printed letters: "We have had supper now & our strength is returning. So far it is a beautiful evening." Then, for the first time – and he was now working on his twenty-second sheet – he began to write in his awkward script, using space recklessly, and the words fairly danced across the small page.

My heart feels real good tonight ... Somehow ... I just feel that I am going to hold you in my arms again. The part that bothers me most of all [is that] if I say I had died the suffering would have been over for me, but just starting for you. When I get home I want to live a good clean life, following the Lord's way. I am going to turn over a new leaf and have a real happy life. I want to be a smart dresser from now on. My hair is even going to have to be combed. I want to trade my truck in for a respectable car.

But most of all I want to change to be a family man. Every one of my hobbies mean nothing to me out here. Just you and the kids and this strange love for God. He has shown me a new way in life & I am sure that I can follow it. You and Geoffrey always did have faith & now so do I. When I get home I want to see your priest and cry in his arms. I think that there will never be a happier family group ever. I want to go to Dad and give him a hug and tell him that I love him. I want to take Mom and set her in my lap & run my fingers through her hair. ... Donna just said to tell you that she loves you & the kids. It's getting dark so I have to go take care of things for a while. Till I get there hug & kiss the kids and tell them Dad is coming home.

They would have to lighten their load. If there was anything they didn't need in either the suitcase or the Bauer bag, it would go into the fire that night. "My flight computer," Brent volunteered. "I'll just hurl it in there. That and my pilot's log."

"But won't you need it to get your licence?"

"Somehow I have the feeling I won't be flying too much when I get out of here."

"You should still save it."

"Okay. I'll burn these blank pages at the end. And maybe there's some extra paper in the back of the diary."

"My Office Practice book, you mean."

"Better save it. Who knows what I'll write. What about this, then? Your hair-curler?"

"Burn it if you want."

"There's no place to plug it in here anyway."

"I'm going to a hairdresser first thing when we get out."

"Don't go to one. We'll order one up. Just like movie stars do. We'll say, hey there, Mr. Bernard, or whatever, you just come up here and do up Donna's hair like it was before."

"You could get yours done too."

"By a *hairdresser*?"

"Sure," Donna said. "Get a razor cut. Get it blow-dried."

"Why not? Shall I burn this then?"

"Your flight computer and my curler. That's fair."

"And whatever else in here we don't need."

"Not the money."

"No."

The fire flared up. Donna watched the flames lick around the edges of her Clairol curling iron, then catch the plastic. The flames were pretty. Pink and blue, like one of those scented logs they sometimes had at home for Christmas. She wished she could pull it out of the fire. Her hair was a mess. But a deal was a deal. And it sure looked nice as it burned.

Just after they had curled up for the night there was a terrible noise from the mountain above.

"Oh God, it's an avalanche," Donna cried. "That snow is going to roll right over us. We shouldn't have made our camp here."

"Wait a minute."

"It's still going on."

The rumble rose to a crescendo, then fell off, then started again.

"It's animals," Brent said.

"Maybe."

"They're fighting or something. Must be some of those sheep. Big horns. Two males, maybe. Listen."

"I hope it is."

"Why?"

"Maybe there's two of them fighting to the death."

"Maybe. Could be, from the sound of it."

"And one of them will be killed, and ..."

"We'll find him tomorrow."

"Already slaughtered for us."

"Roast sheep. That would be good."

"And we could carry out the horns for a trophy."

They slept almost too soundly. During the night the fire spread, and ignited Brent's pants. Right through the leg of the outer pair of jeans, the ones he had borrowed from Donna, it went and through his own jeans underneath. It scorched the sleeve of Don's pyjamas before he felt the heat searing his flesh. The stab of pain woke him, and he beat at the fire with his hands, but the brown and black edges of the holes in the cloth kept spreading, and a knife now seemed to be sticking in his calf. With a yell, he rolled over and into the snow. Finally he smothered it, but he could see the scarlet of his calf under the pyjamas. He got the Blistex from the first-aid kit and smeared it over his flesh.

Tuesday morning the pain was still there, and spreading more lotion on Brent's leg became a part of their daily medical routine, which had included folding back the dressing on Donna's hand and, when they could, changing the bandage and adding more Stop-Bleed. About their most serious injuries they could do nothing. Brent's jaw was now badly infected. Slivers of bone worked their way through the flesh, and in spite of Donna's remonstrations he would push and probe at it, squeezing out the pus. Donna's toes remained numb, even in the hottest part of the day. They were now convinced she would have to lose them. She dared not dwell on what that would mean. The sliding and crawling of the trip had also agitated her hip; it now ached steadily and wakened her through the night as she tried to change positions on the hard ground.

They had laid out pieces of the plane's carpet to act as ground-sheets during the night, but these afforded little comfort. Now, they decided to leave the carpet behind. They would travel as lightly as possible.

The high sun was burning their faces now. Before they set off each day they covered as much of their exposed skin as they could with the Bonne Bell lotion. On their lips it tasted sour and oily. The Blistex gave better protection there.

Tuesday morning's walk seemed easier. Their units of passage sometimes stretched as long as a hundred paces, and once or twice, as they continued down the ridge, they found themselves losing count altogether. But toward noon the terrain turned rough again, scattered with rocks, and offering no apparent natural path. Progress slowed.

By noon, having reached a tree hollowed by rot, they decided to rest. Sitting, they found the sun too hot – they did not cease to wonder at the extremes of the days' heat and the night-time cold – and, even after shedding most of their outer garments, they had to use the rotted tree for shade. They removed their footwear and let it dry. Brent rearranged the layers of his trousers so the holes wouldn't overlap. To his surprise, he found he could now do up the pair of Donna's jeans he wore as his outermost trousers. His waist, always slender, was shrinking.

They moved on. The ridge seemed to be running out, dropping off to the valley below. By mid-afternoon, they could once more see the gap ahead and its promise of green pastures. Their belief kept them going. It was a good day.

That night the tone of Brent's diary changed again. Where he had written before of what he planned to do when he got out – he had never resorted to "if" – he was now offering more specific plans. There was a practicality about it, like a memo. The plans seemed more carefully thought out, less fantasy than firm intention. But there were moments of desperation to it, too. There could *not* be much farther to go.

He began with triumphant news:

We are at the edge of the mountain and the plain is out in front of us. It sure looks beautiful. We had another hard walk again today, but we made it with God's help. We are really going to try to get a hold of you by our anniversary & we think we can. Depending whether you pick us up or we fly home. I want to use that money for my buoyancy compensator [a piece of Scuba equipment] to get a new set of clothes. As you can imagine, these have had it. . . .

If you pick us up I'll have you help me pick out my clothes. I'll get a hold of Dad & he can get you some money. I have to get home. Who is going to build those shelves in your laundry room? Both of us feel so close to being home but we cannot hold back the [urge] to be home now & we get a little homesick. Donna says that when we get back that the three girls are going on a shopping trip to Regina or Winnipeg. I have so darn much love tied up in me right now & we can only talk (Donna & I) about that. If I don't let it out pretty soon I don't know what I'll do. You'd never believe the serenity and respect that I have learned for simple things. When I get back I am really going to take over that business of ours & make it run like clockwork. Within 6 months to a year I'll be running the show & Dad can take it easy. I know in my heart now that love for family & God can make anything happen. When I close my eyes at night now I get happy pictures, not sad ones any more. I am really going to teach you what Donna & I have found. Donna and I are going to talk about today, tomorrow and the future now. So kiss the kids for me. Give yourself a squeeze and please sleep restful tonight with God in your heart & me in your mind.

Chapter Thirteen

Effectively, the search for C-GYVP was over. It stayed on the books, SAR mission number 7-596A, for to declare it over was to declare the plane beyond finding. But after ten days the volunteers had gone back to their workaday lives. Two helicopters remained on call at Bozeman, but there were no leads to follow any more.

In desperation, the family considered a last option: offering a reward. Perhaps a substantial sum, say $10,000, would get some aircraft going again.

Sam Griggs was quick to discourage them.

"I can't tell you how strongly we oppose rewards," he told Brian. "All you can hope to do is get a bunch of amateurs coming in here. They can't possibly look anywhere we haven't looked, and they can't look as well. There's a rule, in fact. You put up a reward and we'll withdraw whatever resources we've got left."

"How come?"

"Because we know what will happen. One of those people will go down. Maybe more than one. And as terrible as it is for you and your family, it's not going to be any better if someone else is lost too."

Brian and Evelyn talked it over. If Griggs was right: there could be another tragedy. Except ... if an aircraft brought in by "amateurs" seeking the reward did go down in the same area, then wouldn't the whole SAR process, whose efficiency impressed them deeply, *have* to begin again? Wouldn't the same careful, rectangle-by-rectangle search be repeated?

In the end, they couldn't do it. Brian went so far as to talk to a lawyer in Livingston about drawing up an offer of reward that would disclaim the family's responsibility for anyone lost in the renewed search. But when they thought about what they'd been through, and the possibility of another family's suffering to the same degree, they decided not to make the offer. It would be, they decided, a bribe for someone else to suffer an ordeal whose dimensions they knew too well. Brian went home.

Wednesday was the longest day.

Below them, as they started to walk, they could see the blackened stumps and trunks of a burned-out forest. It lay between the slopes of the gap they had headed for from the beginning, as bleak as doomsday. The way to the forest was deep in snow, and once again they found themselves counting off their steps, lifting their legs in a grotesque dance, prodding and pulling with their walking sticks, dragging the suitcase and the Bauer bag. The temperature hovered around freezing, and rain dripped from the grey sky, softening the snow and thickening it to slush. The charred forest ahead looked like easier going.

"This will be the last snow," Brent said. "This is the end of it."

Donna struggled on in silence.

The decline of the slope grew more severe. Now they were able to navigate yards at a time by using the suitcase as a toboggan, or simply allowing themselves to slide on their buttocks.

They came to a stream, perhaps four feet wide. Two logs lay across it, and their hearts leapt at the thought they might have been placed there by human hands. They knelt to look for marks. There were none, but in kneeling they saw something that pleased them almost as much: waving in the clear water were fronds of marine grass, a kind of seaweed. It reminded Brent of a fish tank. He pulled a fistful out by the roots, and tried to chew on it. It tasted bland but not unpleasant – certainly better than the berries they'd tried on Monday. Donna tried a mouthful.

"Not bad," she said. "Let's take some with us."

They pulled out as much of the seaweed as they thought they could carry, wringing it out handful by handful and sticking it into the last of their airsickness bags. With two bags full, they decided to move on.

Although the stream would have been easily fordable, they crossed on the two logs.

Just as they reached the other side, they noticed the bird – their whiskey-jack. It must have joined them as they knelt to pick the seaweed.

"That really is a sign," Brent said.

"It's the same one. I'm sure it's the same one we saw back at the plane."

"I'm telling you, it's a sign."

"You don't have to convince me. He's leading us out. I told you. Remember you wanted to get him with a rock?"

"Geez, I wouldn't kill him now for anything."

Still wondering, and with the bird still flying over their heads, sometimes disappearing in front of them but always reappearing just when they expected him least, they continued across the snow. The drizzle of rain persisted. There was less snow now, but the ground was rockier. It was a question of which was harder to negotiate, the snow or the rocks.

Ahead, they could hear what sounded like wind, and yet the trees were still. The sound grew louder. It was water, running water, but much louder than the waterfall they'd encountered earlier. Even before they could see it they became afraid.

"What are we going to do?" Donna asked.

"Have faith," Brent told her. "If there's ever been a time when we should have faith in the Lord, this is it. We'll just walk right to whatever that is ahead and we'll get across it."

"How?"

"We'll just get across. That's all I know."

And when they came to the stream – a river, really, more than eight feet wide and tumbling down the hillside fast enough to throw froth into the air – there was what they had hoped for: a snow bridge. Not just a piece of snow lying between the rocky banks, but a bridge, a genuine, arcing bridge, right in their path. They could have closed their eyes and walked to the river and they would have arrived at its base.

"I'm not sure I believe this," Brent said. "If I ever had any doubts, if I ever doubted for a minute that God wanted us to get out of here I'd kneel right down now and say, 'I'm sorry.'"

"And maybe thanks too."

"Will you *look* at that. That old river just hell-a-hootin' down there, and right across the middle, right where we're going to have to go, a bridge that looks like it came from a miniature golf course or something. That and our bird. Two miracles in one day."

"In one *hour* almost. It's as if the bird was trying to guide us here."

"Maybe he was."

"There he is now. Look at how he's looking at us."

"Do you think anyone's going to believe this when we tell them?"

"You know something?" Donna said. "I don't care. *I* know and *you* know and that's enough."

Whatever the divinity of their guidance, however, they were still faced with a formidable task. The bridge looked terrifyingly flimsy.

"Will it support us?" Donna asked.

"The way things have been going," Brent said, "it's *got* to. I'll go first."

Lying flat on his belly at the near end of the bridge, he pushed the suitcase onto its surface. The snow held. He pushed further. Still safe. He eased his upper body after the suitcase. Soft, but holding. Inch by inch he wriggled ahead. A piece of snow fell silently into the rushing river. The arc was still intact. Over the hump, Brent slithered, letting the suitcase slide to the bottom on the other side. Head first, he eased himself down after it. Careful now. Easy. Made it!

He clambered to his feet.

Now Donna. She tied the belt that held the Bauer bag around her neck and began to crawl on her hands and knees up the bridge. One hand sank into the snow. Her body listed. The bag slipped over the side and dangled over the water.

"Hold as still as you can," Brent said. "Don't move a muscle. Now, lift your weight, go forward until your chin is right in the snow. Don't move toward the edge. That's where it's weak. Just get your chest down into it and let your hand go over the side. That's it. Now reach forward a little. There. Can you feel the strap? Grab ahold of it and just scrinch it up with your fingers. Easy. Bring it up onto the snow. Don't *move* your legs. There. There, you've got it."

The bag was on the snow in front of her now, but in lifting it she'd twisted the belt so much that it had tightened around her neck. She was choking.

"Just let yourself slide down here," Brent said. "This is a kind of island, but we can step from here to the other side. Don't lift your head. Just ease yourself on down here. Gotcha!" He helped her to her feet, taking part of the burden of the Bauer bag with his hand, and beginning to untwist the belt. It loosened. She slipped it over her head. With relative ease, using their walking sticks as props, they stepped to safety and the other side.

They were exhausted.

There seemed to be less snow on this side of the river. Just ahead of them was a long, thin rock, the size of a curling rink. They made their way to its surface and found, to their delight, a small pool of water trapped in a natural basin.

They stripped off their soaking footwear and rolled up their pant-legs. There was no sun yet, but the rain had stopped, and an hour or so would give them a chance to dry out.

They opened the Bauer bag to get portions of meat, and spread some seaweed out on the rock. They washed the food down with rain-water from the basin on the rock. They felt exhilarated.

Replenished, they dug further into the luggage to find toilet articles. With the bar of soap, and using one of the seat-covers as a washcloth, they bathed their hands and their faces up to the hairline, then examined the improvements in the piece of broken mirror. They brushed their teeth with the soap, and then used the surgical soap from the first-aid kit to cleanse around their open wounds. They cleaned under their nails, and washed their faces again in the plentiful water of the basin. Then Brent splashed some Christian Dior after-shave lotion on his face, and Donna used her Charlie perfume. They felt better and cleaner than they had since the plane had crashed.

"You know something, Donna?" Brent was using her name, but with his back turned seemed almost to be talking to himself. "I could die a sober man."

"I don't know what you mean." She had seldom seen him so subdued.

"I'm not sure you could. It goes back to what we believe in at AA. You know? One day at a time. That's what you believe. When you first go there, that's as long as you promise you'll stay away from the booze – one day. That way, well, it's like earlier, when we first started to walk out of here. If we'd ever said we were going to get to the gap in the mountains before we stopped for a rest, we'd never have made it. But by saying we were only to get those few paces, just the ten at a time when we first started, it became something we knew we could do, so we did it. And if a guy who's been drunk for however long – I was nothing compared to some of the guys whose stories I've heard – well, if he told you when he came to the meeting, maybe still shaking from his last bender, that he'd never take another drink for the rest of his life, well, you'd know right then he'd never make it. You know you couldn't make it yourself that way. So that's all you say you'll make: one day. And then the next day you say, well, now I'll get through this one. Like, you never say you're cured. Just that you're off the sauce."

"But you told Cindy –"

"Sure, I told Cindy that I'd quit, and that I wouldn't start again. But the thing is, you *can't* promise that. And all the time you're dry you can't help wondering what it would be like to get drunk just one more time, just once before you died. Listen, drunks have good times, you know. That's the trouble with booze: you think you're having fun, and no matter how long you're away from the stuff you remember some of the fun things you did. You remember the bad things, too. But they don't seem as bad as the good things seem good. You know what I mean? You're always tempted. That's why you go to those meetings, and why members get up and talk about how low they were. Christ, I've heard people you know in Estevan and who you think are pretty respectable citizens, I've heard some of them talk about being so sick in the morning they couldn't even get a cup of coffee down without sneaking a couple of belts to steady their hands and their guts. You hear those stories and you say, well, one more day.

"But you still wonder. What would it be like? What would being drunk again be like?

"And now I don't care any more. I don't want to be drunk – not ever. If a helicopter came right down here now and said, 'Hey there, Brent Dyer, just get on board and we'll booze 'er up all the way back to Estevan,' I'd just say, 'If I have to booze I ain't going. I'm just gonna walk out of here with my little sister-in-law. This little girl here and I are going the rest of the way together, just like we've come this far together, us and the Lord.'

"So that's what I mean. I could die a sober man. I don't guess either of us will ever get closer to death than we have been for the last two weeks—"

"Two weeks and four days."

"—and there wasn't one time when I thought, Jeez, if I'm gonna die I might as well get pissed. Not one time. And up till now I'd always thought I'd have that temptation. But I haven't had it. No, sir. I'll still go to AA when we get back, because I still believe you have to fight one day at a time. But I know something now I never thought I'd live to know."

There was a lot of valley left. It was time to press on. They headed toward the burned forest, where, they figured, there would be plenty of wood for fires. Their confidence was still with them, and so, to their comfort, was their whiskey-jack.

"You think we can get through there without getting lost?" Donna asked.

"I've still got my sense of direction," Brent said. "Besides, we've got a pretty good guy driving."

Brent was in the lead now. They had fallen into that formation as the journey wore on, Brent ahead, breaking trail when necessary, and picking the easiest way through the rocky passages. So it was Brent who came across the mushroom first. One mushroom. Or was it a toadstool? It didn't look like anything he used to find on the prairie. His stomach was not in the best of shape. Pretty bloody awful, to tell the truth—still racked by cramps. But surely there wouldn't be enough poison in this one little mushroom or toadstool or whatever it was to kill him. So, looking slightly furtively over his shoulder at Donna, he picked it and stuffed it in his mouth. He swallowed it in one gulp.

He began to feel guilty. There he'd been, preaching to her on the rock about what a great man he was and now, not even an hour later, he'd bolted down a piece of food they could have shared. No sense lying. He told her the truth. He'd seen it and he'd eaten it. It was a breach of their trust.

Donna forgave him. Anyway, she said, she wasn't sure she wanted to try raw mushrooms right now.

They were at the bottom of the hill. The ridge had led them right to the gap between the mountains, and the valley that stretched out before them, leading to the burned-out forest, was the first level ground they'd walked on. It was still not easy going. Large fallen trees lay all around. Sometimes they would make their way along the trunks, using their sticks and their luggage as balancing poles, and sometimes they'd climb over the sides, but the deadfalls slowed them down and, worse, up ahead and over the standing trees, they could see rain coming. Heavy rain, it looked like. The clouds were closing in the tops of the mountains on either side. It was still clear behind them, but the rain was on a collision path with their own tortuous course.

Just before it hit, they reached a clump of evergreens, tall enough to give them shelter, and offering, beneath their branches, fallen logs to sit on. They were able to rip some of the boughs from the smaller trees, and, by bending over the kindling, to strike a spark in a gas-soaked rag. They stretched their walking sticks between two logs, and rested their feet on them. They tried to relax, but the fire kept flickering down, and one or the other would have to get up to pull a branch or two off the smaller trees, which were fast becoming soggy. The fire was spitting, steaming, but there was no warmth. They pulled their clothes around their heads, but there was little comfort. The drizzle continued, and their spirits plummeted from the heights of their elation at the snow bridge. Brent decided to share a discovery he'd made earlier.

"You know that rock where I was talking about how I'd never drink again?" he said.

"Uh huh."

"There was something else."

"Oh?"

"All the time I was talking to you I was scratching away at the top with my stick, you know, just scraping away there."

Silence.

"You know what I saw there?"

"What?"

"Red. Red stains. Right near that basin. Deep red. You know what that means?"

Silence.

"Seriously, Donna, you know what that means? Iron! Iron ore! We can stake it when we get out of here. We'll be rich!"

No reply.

"Don't you hear me, Donna?" He was getting excited. "Iron ore. Ours!"

Donna raised her head.

"Big deal," she said. "Big fucking deal."

After half an hour the rain began to let up, but they could see heavier, blacker clouds approaching. The charred forest, with its promise of more solid shelter, might be reachable. They decided to make a break for it.

"What about the fire?" Donna said.

"Let 'er burn," Brent said. "A big Jesus forest fire would be the best signal we could send up."

The rain was getting even thicker now, falling in drops that felt like cupfuls against their skin, soaking through all the layers of their clothing. They stumbled into the partial shelter of the blackened trees only to be greeted by a nightmare of fallen logs strewn over the rugged ground like giant pick-up sticks. It was hard even to move among them, and the dead trees that still stood offered less shelter than they'd hoped. They sought out a rock, less than three feet high, but a good five feet across. In its lee, they tried to build a fire, first wiping dry and stacking whatever twigs they could find, then covering them with the ends of the biggest logs they could move around. They had little success. The kindling caught, and some of the smaller wood, but the big logs, even the ends, would not catch. The savagery of the forest fire had sucked the combustible material from their wood.

The rain continued, a downpour now. Cupping his notebook under his jacket, Brent scrawled a few words to Cindy: "We have been fighting snow, rivers and mountains, and now it starts to rain."

The bird that had become so important to them, the whiskey-jack, was nowhere to be seen.

Cold, miserable and drenched to their skins, they had reached the end of their courage.

Brent raised his face to the storm.

"Lookit," he said. "We can't take any more. If You want to end it for us now, we quit. That's it. If that's what You want, You win. Otherwise, please stop this goddamn rain."

And it stopped. Not instantly, as if a tap had been turned off, but so quickly did the downpour become a shower, the shower a drizzle, the drizzle a drip, and then so completely did it stop that he felt as if he'd commanded it. No, not commanded it, *asked* for it. And it had happened. The rain had stopped, and now, as they looked up to the night sky, they were sure they saw a star.

They began to stoke their fire again.

News of the missing townspeople had cast a pall over Estevan's Consolidated High School. On the Monday after the crash, Ron Coulter, who had been Donna's boyfriend for as long as anyone could remember, had been seen sobbing over his books in the library. The next day he'd been gone, to take part in the search. "I thought he'd be on his own," his sister Della had said to her boyfriend Norman Mack. "But everyone cares."

The school paper, the ECOMS, carried the sombre news: "Reported missing – Donna Johnson, grade 12, and her father. . . . The students and staff of this school extend their sincerest hopes and prayers that they may be found and returned safely to the family and friends who are nearest and dearest to them."

It had affected everyone. Harvey Hackney, Donna's Office Practice teacher, had set out maps of Idaho and Montana in his classroom one day and they'd all tried to will themselves to know where the plane might be. Giselle Bausche, teacher of Christian ethics, had offered a special prayer. But it hit the students hardest. They gathered in the hallways or, after school, at the Canada Café or the Dairy Queen or Gaines Gas Bar, where some of the boys worked pumping gas. "Not Donna," they would say. "Donna is just too *beautiful*." There was no jealousy in their voices.

Kathy Muirhead and Brent Johner were the first to suggest raising money. Kathy was the younger sister of Jack Muirhead, who'd been on the search, and Brent sometimes bowled with Brent Dyer, but their personal connections had little to do with their desire to get involved; in one way or another almost all the students had known Brent or Donna; Kathy and Brent just happened to have the opportunity, they said.

The opportunity was a radio show called *1:05 Live*, which Kathy and Brent hosted on CJSL, the local station, every Saturday. They decided to use the show to ask for funds to help pay for the search for their missing friends; they would open the telephone lines. They told the station of their plans and checked them out with the Dyer and Johnson families. Everyone told them their idea was fine. Then someone – it was difficult to say who, because everyone seemed to be in on the plans – suggested selling tickets to a dance, so people could get something instead of just giving their money, and someone else said why not two dances, so the adults wouldn't have to listen to rock music, and the whole thing just took off. Tommy Abraham volunteered his orchestra for the adult dance at the Legion, and John Deadlock, a former radio man who now served on town council and who knew Brent through his own work with AA, said he'd be master of ceremonies. Jokers Wild, a rock group from the school, volunteered to play for the young people, and CFSL, the Weyburn station, offered sound equipment. Tracy Jackson, who was a majorette with Donna, said her mother, who ran the A & W, would help out by putting signs up. At times there seemed almost more willing helpers than there were jobs to do.

No one could believe the response to the radio show. Kathy's father called in with $125 from the Legion, of which he was president, and a four-year-old child they could hardly hear on the phone pledged two dollars. Pace Aviation rounded up $504 from their employees and Ward Mowry, a teacher at the school, gave twenty dollars from his own pocket. Someone called from Winnipeg – they hadn't known they could be heard that far away – with $500. A man from Ontario, driving through, called from a pay-phone with twenty dollars. Someone else was listening on his car radio while he waited for a tow-truck and when the driver told him there'd be no charge he handed him twenty and said give it to those kids on the radio.

They'd wondered if they could keep the lines busy from 1:05 until two, but it was after four when they finally went off the air and they'd raised more than $10,000.

Kathy and Brent, who were both sixteen years old, were deeply moved. "We knew this was the best town in Canada," Kathy said as they wrapped up the show, "but even we didn't know how good it was."

They scheduled the dance for May 24, traditionally a Canadian holiday in honour of the birthday of Queen Victoria.

Chapter Fourteen

They saw their first sign of other human beings shortly after ten o'clock on Thursday morning. It was nineteen days since they had left Estevan for Boise. The sign was a footprint. With crinkles in the heel, it looked like a hiking boot. It was one of the most beautiful things they had ever seen in their lives. Beside the footprint was a lump of horse manure. The horse manure was beautiful, too. Brent pushed at the footprint with the toe of his suede shoe. It was hard, set in the ground as if in cement. He pushed at the horse manure. It was dry.

"Last year's," he said.

"Who cares?" Donna said.

They had been walking a little over an hour. When they had wakened in the burned forest a light rain had been falling. It had been nothing like the downpour of the night before, and it had soon stopped. The sky was clear now, and the temperature was cool. It felt like spring.

They had walked away from the burned-out area toward what they had assumed was a green meadow when they saw it from the mountaintop. But it was not a meadow at all, just gentler land. To their right they had seen a pile of logs, which, although neatly arranged, seemed to have no natural reason for being there. Beside the logs ran what could easily have been a trail, and beside that, the footprint. Upon closer inspection, the logs appeared to have been cut by a chain-saw.

They turned onto the faintly indicated trail. It stayed on level ground, wending its way along a single contour of the terrain. To either side they saw tangled vegetation, but the outlines of the trail itself became clearer and clearer as they moved, and there were more prints in the ground, left by both humans and horses. The walking was easy.

The trail, marked by stumps, led into stands of trees. They saw initials carved into a trunk: a *G*, an *H*, a *B*.

"You know something," Brent said. "That means there's more than one person around here. No one cuts his girlfriend's initials where she's not even going to see them."

"No *kidding!*" Donna said. It was hard to hide her high spirits.

"No, wait a minute. This means we're not on some path a guy has cut for himself and then forgotten about. This is a trail people *use*."

Donna smiled with him.

"More than that, it means there's more than one farm near here. No one carves initials on a tree for his sister."

"Maybe they do up here."

"Anyway, we know it's ranching country. That's elementary, my dear Johnson. The horse shit."

"It can also mean we're a long way from where they live. You know the Beggs? They sometimes push their cattle down to Roche Percee, and that's thirty miles from their place."

"Well, if worse comes to worst, we'll walk thirty miles. Isn't that how far Ron was going to walk for his hockey team? Up to Benson?"

"Ron's in better shape than we are."

"I feel right now as if I could walk thirty miles."

"I hope we're not going to have to."

Donna started moving ahead. Even now, on the fifth day of their pilgrimage, they were taking rest periods, usually every hundred paces, but they stopped for less time than when they'd started. Just long enough to catch their breath. Now Donna was walking almost steadily, reversing the order of parade they'd maintained throughout their march.

Brent objected. "I can't keep up with you," he said. "If you stay behind we'll be more even."

"Sure."

He was switching the suitcase from side to side, dividing its load as best he could between his arms. The signs of human life grew more frequent: axe marks on a tree, a cigarette butt, a clearing where the grass appeared to have been trampled flat.

"Maybe kids come here," Brent said. "And if that's true they'll be here soon. It's almost June, and school will be out."

"I'm not waiting."

"Me neither."

They began to imagine what kind of people they might come across.

"I hope it's a big fat farm wife," Donna said. "One who makes her own bread and has cows for fresh milk."

They decided to stop. Even to themselves, their reasons were not clear. They were so near. A house, a farm, a village could have lain around any bend in their path, appeared over any ridge. And yet, and yet. They were so high on the anticipation of what they now knew was about to happen that they had no need – no urgent need – for the experience itself. It was close to noon. They would pause for lunch.

They came to an open area, snow-free and verdant. As they began to settle, they noticed ground squirrels – gophers – frisking in the grass.

"I think I'll just snare me one of those," Brent said.

He began to dismantle the extension cord that had served so many purposes. First he unwound its two strands, as he had with the wire from the plane's engine, but this time more slowly and carefully. He joined the two strands in a careful splice. With the tiny jackknife, and spending nearly half an hour at the task, he whittled away, first the clear plastic coating and then the coloured wrapping of the wire. One of the gophers stood sniffing the air, appearing to observe his labours. Now he had a thin strand of almost twenty feet long. He tied a knot in one end, and slipped the other end through to form a loop. Then he crawled over to one of the gopher holes, put his snare around its perimeter, and sat with his back against a tree to wait.

Donna, sitting idly, thumbed through her father's wallet. There were some notes with figures on them. Business notes? She wondered. The night before they left she'd helped him do some calculations on stocks and bonds. They'd enjoyed it, he smiling at her arithmetic and she proud to be able to work with real money instead of school projects. His Chargex card. How many presents had he bought her with that? What good was it now? *Donald Johnson*, it read. There was no Donald Johnson now. Finally, the purple card proclaiming his membership in the Estevan branch of the Order of the Elks. For a reason she couldn't determine, the Elks card hit her especially hard. He used to take the family there on special occasions: in a basement restaurant for members only, the Elks served the best steak and lobster in Estevan. There would be no more dinners with him there, no more special occasions.

And then she knew. As close as they had been in life, she had been even closer to him in death. For the past nineteen days, her father had lived through her. Now, so close to returning to the land of the living, she knew that finally she was leaving him behind. He would, she promised herself, be a part of her always. But it would never be like this again.

A gopher was sticking his head up. Brent pulled the wire. Too quick. He missed it. He reset his trap, sat back again. Ten minutes more. Another head. He waited. Shoulders emerged. Now ... he pulled. He had it. He began reeling the wire in. The gopher struggled. He pulled sharply on the wire. Wrong angle. The gopher wriggled free. He looked up at Donna with a grin.

"Guess we just weren't meant to have that pesky little bugger," he said. "Time to go."

They got up, arranged their clothing, closed up the luggage and set off down the trail once more.

Behind them in the grassy clearing, unnoticed, lay the toy jack-knife.

They kept feeling better and better. There was a small brook now beside the path, and at their leisure they would stop to sip. They were making good time. They heard grasshoppers, a prairie sound up here in the rocky hills.

Brent said: "They eat locusts in Africa, you know."

Donna kept walking. They were in thick woods now but the path was more and more clearly marked. They came to a stream with a manmade if rustic log bridge. One of the logs was under water. It didn't matter. They slipped off their footwear and threw it to the opposite bank. Their walking sticks and the luggage – who cared now if the gas bottle broke? – followed. They clambered barefoot across the submerged log, squealing at the cold water. This cold was nothing like what they had felt so deeply and so long. It was almost sweet.

A sign was nailed to a post on the other side of the river. Brent waited until Donna got her shoes and socks back on, so they could read it together. NO MOTOR VEHICLES BEYOND THIS POINT, it ordered.

"Okay," said Brent. "We'll leave our four-by-four here."

"It means the other way," said Donna.

They were getting giddy with the joy.

The trail divided, one fork obviously more heavily travelled than the other. They chose the popular route. More animal dung. Then a corral beside the path. It was empty, but obviously ready to use. Then motorcycle tracks. Then signs of campfires. A pickle jar. Another hour of walking, limping, hurting but now not pausing for rest stops at all. Another corral. Another sign: BURN OR CARRY OUT YOUR REFUSE. A solid bridge, with heavy beams bolted together. They lay down on it and stretched out in the sun, wanting to sleep, but unable to.

"If there's a sign on the other side of this bridge that says twenty miles to the nearest town or whatever," said Brent, "we'll walk it. Even if it means we walk all night."

But then he had to stop again. Cramps. Bad cramps. He was bent over. It was half an hour before he was ready to go on. A light rain started to fall. Just a sprinkle. They turned a corner and there, spread out before them, were . . . .

Buildings.

One, two, three, four . . . ten, small rectangular log buildings, with tin roofs, laid out in a formation that was almost military in its neatness, then a group of larger log constructions and, on a small rise overlooking the whole site, the largest of all, also made of logs and roofed with tin.

And among the whole, not a sign of human life. Just two white goats, moving idly along the neat rows.

Brent and Donna moved toward the largest building. They circled it. A door was open.

"Hello," they cried. "Hello! Hello!"

Down in one of the smaller buildings, Elmer Swanson turned to his son Alfred.

"I suppose it's more of those hippies," he said.

The Swansons didn't like people sponging off them. Elmer had bought the mine site, called Livingston, after the brothers who'd staked it nearly a century before, in 1960, when most people had thought it was mined out. Over the years, men had taken more than $9 million in gold, silver, copper, lead, and zinc out of the Livingston Mine, and in the 1920's, at the height of the metals boom, as many as 128 miners had lived in the neat row of bunkhouses. But the company had gone into receivership in 1930. When Elmer, then a California logger, had acquired it, the camp was empty and run down. He'd moved up right after, with his wife Shirley and three-year-old son Alfred.

Over the years, the Swansons had fixed up the site again, repairing the bunkhouses, and Elmer had worked on the roads and spent a lot of time writing letters to the government, saying if only they'd build a railroad up to the mine it could really get going again. Times had changed, he kept pointing out. There was still plenty of zinc in the claim, now worth thirty-seven cents a pound: in the old days, people thought so little of zinc they used it for back-fill. But no one would listen.

During the winters the world left the Swansons alone. The nearest town, Challis, was almost fifty miles away, and in spite of Elmer's work on his end, the road was all but impassable in tough weather. There were often stretches of six months or more when they saw no one. But when the weather turned good, as it was beginning to now, more and more people had started to drop in. Most of them were young, and many of them needed either haircuts or brassieres, and Elmer wasn't fond of them. The mine was his home.

Now he heard something up at the cookhouse. It couldn't be Shirley. She was in their living quarters, working on her novel, the book that one day he knew would make her famous and stop the people in Challis from making remarks about her when she went into town to shop. He told Alfred they'd better go have a look. They started to move up the hill.

Brent and Donna had found food. A loaf of fresh bread, and honey and dried prunes and some oatmeal and, most miraculous of all, a pitcher of milk. When Elmer and Alfred Swanson arrived at the cookhouse it was as if two of the bears had got home before Goldilocks had gone to bed. They were stuffing themselves.

For a moment, all four stood in frozen silence, staring at each other. Then Elmer spoke:

"Who . . . who are you?"

"We've been in an airplane crash," said Brent.

"Oh sure," said Alfred.

"No, I'm not kidding," Brent said. "I'm Brent Dyer from Estevan, Canada, and this is Donna Johnson and we've been in a crash. Can you help us?"

"You're those Canadians?" Elmer asked. He'd heard something on the radio about the missing plane.

"Oh Jesus, yes," Brent said, and then he stumbled toward Elmer and collapsed against his body. And Elmer, feeling odd, wrapped his arms around the sobbing young man and held him, while Donna, who had been feeling guilty about their invasion of the food supply, stood by and grinned.

The four of them went down to roust out Shirley.

Brent regained his composure. "This sounds stupid," he said, "but what state are we in?"

"Probably shock," said Elmer.

"But which, like, *United* State?"

"Oh, Idaho. You're in the White Cloud Mountain of Idaho," Elmer said and proceeded to tell them about Challis, and how far they were from any real civilization. "Where did you think you were?"

"Well, we figured Idaho. But it might have been Montana. We can hardly remember the crash. Challis sounds right, eh, Donna?"

She told them about having seen the Challis Vikings sign, and that being one of their last memories.

"The high school football team," said Alfred.

"But didn't you have maps?" Elmer asked.

"Norm, our pilot, must have walked off with the ones that might have helped us. He left on the second day. We don't know where he went. Donna's father was killed. All we had were maps of places we'd flown over on the way here. We knew where Livingston was, but not where we'd gone from there."

"This is Livingston Mine, but it hasn't got anything to do with Livingston, Montana. I can't figure out how you found us."

"We just walked where the Lord told us," Brent said. "We knew we'd reach something."

The Swansons looked at them curiously.

"The Lord showed us how to get out. He kept us alive and He brought us out."

Shirley, too, had difficulty believing who the young couple really were. But there was something about their accents – a round sound to *ou*, which made them sound as if they'd been *oot* in the mountains, and a habit of saying "eh" at the end of their sentences – that convinced her. She offered them food. What would they like?

"Anything you've got," Donna said.

"I guess most of all," Brent said, "I'd like a cup of coffee first."

So Shirley put a kettle on and started bringing food out of the cupboards. They'd had a taste of the bread and honey and some milk up at the cookhouse, but this was real food. Hot food.

The first thing she served them was spinach. Brent put a gob of butter on top, and as much salt as he dared, and wolfed down his full portion. Donna ate more slowly. Then came some warmed over chicken and rice – delicious – and rhubarb pie, and fruit juice. They must have drunk two cans of fruit juice each, and then a tin of plums.

"Don't eat too much," Shirley said.

"Don't worry," they said.

All five of them were full of questions, Brent and Donna about what the world had known or assumed about their fate – the Swansons knew little – and the three people of the mountains about how they'd stayed alive, and where they'd walked from. About the first set of questions, the young people were reticent.

"We had some candy on board that we ate at first," Donna said, "and when that ran out we ate moss and berries and stuff."

"Mushrooms," Brent added. "We found some mushrooms, and this seaweed stuff in one of the streams."

About their walk they were much more expansive, describing in detail their path down the mountain ridge and through the burned-out forest and onto the trail.

"That's the trail that goes up to Walker Lake," Shirley said. "Tough country. Hikers use it in the summer."

"How far does it go?"

"About seven miles. You'd have gone farther than that, though."

"How far?"

"Hard to say," said Elmer. "From what you say it could be about ten or twelve miles straight across, but that's not allowing for up and down. Even in good weather and with all the right equipment it might take someone a couple of days, maybe more, to get where you got. The shape you're in it's a wonder you made it as quick as you did."

"It wasn't easy," said Donna.

Most of all they wanted to use a telephone, to call their families. The Swansons had no phone, but there was a family down the way, the Bensons, who had one.

"I don't want to trouble you," Brent said, "but could you maybe run down there in that Wagoneer I saw parked outside and get them to call our families." He started writing out a list of names and numbers.

"No trouble at all," said Shirley. But no one moved.

Brent and Donna were getting edgy. These people were kind, and they'd been more than generous with their food, and now the warmth of the house was beginning to spread through their bones, but they didn't seem to want to let them go.

Brent mentioned the phone again.

"Don't you want to clean up?" Shirley said.

They did, of course. But the phone?

"Well, the Bensons probably can't reach your folks anyway. Phones aren't too good up here in the hills. But they could call the sheriff and he could come and get you."

"Okay. That would be great."

"Or we could take you down there."

"Anything, we just want to call."

"What about a shower?"

It was getting ridiculous.

"Look, if we went down to your neighbours, we could come back here to spend the night. You've been really good to us."

"We don't get many real visitors, you know. Just those hippies that want to live for nothing in the bunkhouses."

Finally, Shirley left to go to the Bensons.

Donna went to take a shower. She couldn't believe the dirt that came off her. The water was black as it ran down the drain. The more she rinsed, the blacker it seemed to grow. It must be coming out of her pores. Scrubbing was hard; the cut in her hand started to hurt again, although it didn't open. There wasn't much light in the bathroom, but she didn't want to look in a mirror anyway. She still felt dirty when she walked out to tell Brent it was his turn.

Brent couldn't get clean either. And before he could really get a lather up the water turned icy. The overhead tank, heated by the camp's generating system, was empty. He joined Donna and the Swansons in the main room. Donna was stretched out on her back on a fold-away cot. They offered Brent the most comfortable chair, and when he'd leaned back Elmer offered him some of his pipe tobacco and a cigarette paper. He rolled a smoke, his first since the seven he'd chainsmoked at the plane, and held it vertically to keep the pipe tobacco from falling out as he sucked the nicotine down into the depths of his lungs. Great! But he'd sure like to talk to Cindy.

Shirley Swanson arrived back with her neighbours in tow, and once more they had to tell their stories.

When the sheriff got there, at last, Brent gave the snare he'd made that morning to the Swansons as a souvenir.

IV
The Survivors
May 24 and after

Chapter Fifteen

Sid Teuscher, the sheriff of Custer County, didn't know when he'd heard anyone chattering so much in the back of his car. The sheriff is a big man. Sometimes he livens up the Fourth of July celebrations in Challis by putting a couple of planks across his chest and having a car drive over them, and once he hitched a rope to a pick-up truck and dragged it for most of a block by his teeth. So the people in the back of his car are almost always quiet. But the young man he was driving back down the lumpy, twenty-four-mile road to town was something else.

They were about half way back to Challis now, from Elmer Swanson's place, and he didn't think the young man, Brent Dyer, had stopped talking once. "How far does this radio reach?" he'd ask. "How long till we get to a phone?" And then he and the young lady, Miss Johnson, would start planning what they were going to eat.

"Is there a Dairy Queen in Challis?" Brent asked.

Ron Wardly, the Search and Rescue man who was riding alongside the sheriff in the front, said, no, he didn't think there was. Why?

"I could sure go for a hot fudge sundae."

"With nuts," said Donna.

"I'll see what we can do," Wardly said.

They must be pretty amazing kids, Teuscher thought, to have walked out of there alive. He'd radioed ahead and told Dr. Maxwell to be ready to meet them. A search plane had left Challis before 7:30, not long after Teuscher had started up for the mine, but according to the radio reports he was getting now they hadn't been able to find the wreck. He turned to ask Brent again about the location. And once again Brent told him about the canyon, with the larger mountain on its northeastern edge, and the lake on the other side of the rim, and tried his best to retrace the path they'd covered.

There was a long pause. The car bounced along for a couple of miles in relative silence before Brent spoke again.

"You're really going in there to get the body, eh?"

"Have to, son. Maybe you could show us by helicopter tomorrow. If you're up to flying, that is."

Another long pause. Then:

"Sheriff, is there any law against ... I mean, well, we ate some of Don's flesh."

Brent was having trouble talking now, and Donna seemed to be starting to cry. Wardly reached over from the front seat to hand Donna a Kleenex.

Teuscher spoke: "There's no law against it, son."

"Well ... is it wrong?"

"There's only two people who can answer that, Brent, and you're both sitting in the backseat of this car right now. You two and whatever God you believe in. I think you know the answer yourself and you don't need Sid Teuscher to tell you what it is."

There was a newsman on the line, from some paper in Chicago. Brent couldn't believe it. He'd just picked up the phone in the doctor's office and was trying to get the operator to call Cindy, when a voice came on and started asking him questions.

"Are you one of the survivors?"

"Get off the phone will you?"

"Are you one of the people who was in the crash?"

"Get off the phone."

"– just wanted to know if you –"

"Will you get off the fucking phone?" He was yelling now. "I'm trying to call my *wife*."

Cindy screamed. There was no other way to describe it. Just one great "*yeea-aaah!*"

The scream was so loud that Donna could hear it coming through the phone across the room in the doctor's office.

In Estevan, Rob and Karen Peters came running over from next door to see what was wrong.

She'd been watching television. When the phone rang she hadn't even wondered who it was. And when the voice had said, "Hello, Cindy, it's Brent," she hadn't been able to make any sound at first. Then Brent said, "What's the matter? Don't you recognize your own husband?" And she'd just rolled her head back and screamed, letting all the anguish of the nineteen days of waiting come out. Brent was safe and Donna was safe. Her dad hadn't made it, and ... Cindy broke down so completely that Bob Peters had to pick up the phone and tell Brent what was happening.

When Cindy got back on the line, Brent told her to wait right there, he'd be making some more calls. Cindy didn't want him to leave the phone – she didn't ever want to be out of touch with him again – but he said he'd call back in half an hour. Wait there and keep the phone clear.

Donna seemed suddenly timid. Brent had started to place the call to Evelyn and he was gesturing Donna to come to the phone, but Donna was hesitant.

"You talk to her," she said.

"She'll want to hear from you."

"You call."

"You think she'll be mad at you?"

"It's hard to explain. You, you place the call. I'll talk to her, but you place the call."

When he got through, Brent had to tell Evelyn that Don was dead, but that because of his gift of the jacket Donna was alive. Marie came to the phone for a minute, and Brent repeated the news, and then Donna took over the phone in Challis.

"Will you come and get me, Mom?" she said.

Brent told her to tell everyone to go to Cindy's. Evelyn said she'd call Brian, and then she and Marie would leave.

Ron was out, his mother said, probably at the dance. When Brent and Donna explained as much as they could of the news, Mrs. Coulter told them about how the kids had all got together to raise money to get the search going again. When they hung up Brent turned to Dr. Maxwell.

"Ten thousand dollars," he said. "They raised ten thousand dollars just to try to find us."

"That must be some kind of town," Dr. Maxwell said.

"Will you accept a call from ... ?"

"Brent, is it really you?"

Jimmy was in his pyjamas. He'd bathed and was ready for bed. His wife, Evylene, was still in the bathroom. He was glad he'd taken a heart pill earlier.

"I'm safe. Donna and I walked out. Don is dead. Norm is ... Norm walked away and ... he must be dead, but we're all right."

"Talk to your mother. Here she is now. Oh, Brent."

Jimmy had to sit down. Two miracles, he thought. His son had been returned to him twice: once from his troubles with liquor, and now from the valley of death itself. He wept in joy. Evylene was crying too, as she handed him back the phone. Brent was trying to tell him as much as he could about what had happened.

"We're all right," he kept saying. "I lost twenty-six pounds and Donna lost sixteen, but we're okay."

"What did you eat?"

"Moss. Stuff like that."

"Is that all?"

"Sure."

"You sound funny. What did you eat?"

"Moss. Some candy. Berries. You know."

"That's bullshit, Brent. You ate Don, didn't you?"

"Yes."

"I thought so. Don't say anything about it until I get there."

"Why? We didn't do anything wrong. We did what the Lord –"

"I know you didn't. You did the right thing. Just don't say anything until I get there."

"When will you be here?"

"Just as soon as I can."

Phyllis Larter, the politician's wife, answered the call from Mike Ferguson of the Montana Aeronautics Division. "Bob's in the shower right now," she said. "Can I take a message, or can I have him call you back."

"For news like this," Ferguson said. "He won't mind being wet."

"I'm afraid the news isn't good, Mrs. Pischke," said the deep voice from Montana. "But we'll start searching again tomorrow. He could be alive out there."

Dry eyed, Sharon went into the bedroom to look at her sleeping sons.

True to his word, Ron Wardly, the SAR man, brought them hot fudge sundaes – and hamburgers, and chips and milk. They drank three glasses of milk each, but neither of them could finish all the chips. Dr. Maxwell said they were in remarkable shape, considering. Brent's jaw and Donna's toes were the most serious problems. He stuck a needle in Brent's chin to anesthetize it before he poked in, and just as the freezing was taking hold he asked Brent if he was a drinking man.

"No, sir, I'm not," Brent said. "I quit drinking a long time ago with the help of the Lord and I'm not going to start now."

The doctor said he'd been going to offer Brent a big drink of rum, thought he might have one himself, in fact. Brent said he'd rather have a coffee. So they made him a coffee while the rest of the examination went on, and then the doctor asked, "Well, are you a smoking man?"

"I quit that three weeks ago," Brent said.

"No, you didn't," said Dr. Maxwell, with his red, outdoorsman's face crinkling into a smile, and he stuck a cigarette into Brent's mouth and offered him a light. It was maybe the best cigarette Brent had ever had in his life, a real smoke, not like the pipe tobacco he'd had back with those people on the mountain.

They took Donna into another part of the clinic for X-rays. There might be some bones broken in her wrist and hand, they said, but they could leave that till she got home. Her toes would be okay. They had to cut some of the dead skin away, and they told her they'd start to hurt her soon, but she wouldn't lose her toes. She was very lucky, they said.

At home in Weiser, Idaho, Jimmy Robertson and his wife Myrtle heard on the ten o'clock news that two people had walked out of the crash. The news gave no names, or if it did, the Robertsons didn't hear them. Mr. Robertson called the switchboard at KTVB but no one seemed to know, so he drove down to the Weiser sheriff's office. There, he was told to call Sid Teuscher's office, and Teuscher's despatcher told him, as presumably she had told the reporter from Chicago, to call the clinic. Dr. Maxwell's nurse called Brent to the phone.

"Where the hell is Weiser?" he could hear Brent say in the background, and when he finally came on the line it took Mr. Robertson a full minute to make his own identity clear.

"We were wondering if you still wanted the dog," he said.

"Whoo boy, the dog!" Brent said. "Do we ever!"

Mr. Robertson said he'd go home and pick up the puppy and they'd be in Challis the next afternoon.

There was no one home at Jimmy Dyer's, although the door was open and from inside the television blared, so Bob Larter swung his Chrysler back onto the street and went down to Brent and Cindy's house. He had to park down the street because of the number of cars that filled the double driveway and were lined up outside. There must have been two dozen people inside, milling about, making drinks, distributing coffee. Cindy held court in the kitchen, her long blonde hair in disarray, her eyes red from tears, but greeting everyone by name. Jimmy and Evylene Dyer stood beaming beside her. Cousins and neighbours stood and sat in groups. The two Dyer boys ran whooping everywhere. On an armchair in the living room, Evelyn Johnson, as well groomed as always, balanced a cup of coffee; her eyes were clear.

Most of the conversation, as nearly as Larter could figure out, was about who would be driving down, and when they'd leave. Lists of possible cars and drivers were circulating. Young Jack Muirhead said he was ready to leave at once – they could drive all night – and others agreed. With at least two able-bodied drivers in each car, they could spell each other. Wouldn't take much more than twelve hours. Road maps were spread on the coffee table in the living room.

Bob sought out Jimmy Dyer.

"Going down?"

"I wouldn't miss it. It's a miracle isn't it?"

"It's incredible. Have you talked to Brent?"

"Twice now. He called me at home – collect, the little bugger – and then I talked to him again from here. They sound okay."

"Jimmy, I'm happy for you."

"It's too bad about Don."

"And Norm. Does anyone know what happened to him?"

"Brent said he walked off really early. Couldn't talk. They figure he's dead for sure since he hasn't shown up. You knew him, didn't you?"

"Used to fly me around. Hell of a pilot!"

"Bob, I don't know if we can ever thank you. You and all the other people who did so much for us all. I never knew how many friends we had. You know, well, I won't tell you his name, because you know him, but there's one really prominent man in town I never even knew was an AA and I'd hardly spoken to him in years. He just took to coming round every night to talk to me and Evylene. He'd just sit for a while, and see if we needed anything. Never talked about Brent being missing or anything."

"I'm just happy it turned out the way it has for Brent and Donna."

"Brent said it was God. He told me they had signs from God to guide them out."

"I guess they prayed a lot."

"I think we all did. Know what I'm going to do as soon as I get back here?"

"Probably buy Brent another present."

"Oh, yeah, I might. I'd like to. But there's something else. There's this kid came around just today asking for a job. He's not all there, you know? Doesn't read too well. He's been fired from where he was working. Showed up drunk one morning, and they told him to get lost. He told me he just wanted another chance. And, by God, I'm going to give him one. I'll find something for him. Washing cars or something. Yes, sir, I'll do that."

"You're a good man, Jimmy Dyer."

"I'm a lucky man. I've got my son back. I thank the good Lord for that."

"You'll really have him back soon. I'd better go. You know that dance is on."

"Holy Christ, I stone forgot about that. Those kids who got the show going on the radio. Will you tell them thanks for me?"

"I sure will, Jimmy."

"Bob?"

"Yes."

"They ate Don."

"They –"

"They had to. Brent told me. I told him to shut up about it till I got there. Evelyn doesn't know yet. But I thought I should tell you."

"That was the right thing to do, Jim."

The place to take his two young charges, Sheriff Teuscher decided, was the Village Inn. There'd be room there, with the hunting and fishing seasons not yet under way, and the food in the restaurant was the best in Challis. Just as important, Tom and Donna Butts, the proprietors, had children of their own not much younger than Brent and Donna and would know how to look after them and give them some peace from the reporters who would be sure to start arriving soon. The youngsters would need rest more than they'd need to talk to the press; there was certainly no need to get into the matter of what they'd had to do to stay alive, certainly not before they'd had a chance to see their families.

The Butts would be more than pleased, they said. And don't worry about people prying. Remember when Nelson Rockefeller had been in there for a holiday? No one had bothered him.

The sheriff drove Brent and Donna to the Village Inn.

"Is there a phone here?" Brent asked.

"Out here in the lobby," said Tom Butts. "But don't be too long."

Brent looked surprised.

"I'm just kidding," said Tom. "Make all the calls you want. Anything we can do for you, just let us know. Donna's fixed up a real nice room for you."

The sheriff asked if they'd mind talking some more to two of the SAR people who'd flown into town. They'd want to go out for the wreckage early the next morning.

Once again, Brent described the crash site as best he could, and drew a map of the canyon. The two SAR people left.

"Geez, they're nice," Brent said.

Donna agreed. "Everyone here is just unreal."

The people at the Legion seemed to know something important had happened even before Larter got to the stage. There were people there from both dances now. Music had stopped at the school just after ten o'clock, and the older kids who wanted to keep going had come to join their elders and finish the evening to the more sedate sounds of Tommy Abraham and his orchestra.

Larter had a hard time making his way through the crowd. "Have you heard something?" . . . "Is there news?" The expression on his face must have given it away. He whispered to John Deadlock, the MC, and John asked Tommy if Bob could speak after the next number. He borrowed a hand mike from Deadlock.

"Ladies and gentlemen," he said, and his years on the hustings helped him hold back for just the right dramatic effect. "Half an hour ago, Brent Dyer phoned his father. He and Donna are –"

The ovation was the loudest he'd ever heard. They were jumping in the air, yelling and screaming and pounding each other on the back. The band started trying to play a tune and then the players simply joined in the fray . . . honking their instruments like horns of revelry.

He had to quiet them down. There was still the rest of the news. He hated to do it. Let them enjoy the good news, *only* the good news. But before it could get totally out of hand, he cleared his throat into the microphone and raised his hand. Donald Johnson, he said, had been killed, and it looked as if Norm Pischke had been, too.

There was a moment of quiet, and then people began to murmur. No one really knew what to say. The band was silent.

Young Norman Mack came up to the stage and gestured to Larter. Larter gave him the microphone.

"I think," he said, "that Brent and Donna would like us all to say a prayer now." And then he broke into sobs. John Deadlock finished the prayer.

At Cindy's house, the cars were getting ready to leave. A neighbour, Isobel Baril, had agreed to sit with the boys so Cindy could go. There were lots of drivers: Ron and Brian and young Jack Muirhead would start off. They should be there by mid-afternoon.

Jay came to sit on Evelyn's lap. She hugged him.

"Are you going to get my daddy?" he said.

"Yes, dear," said Evelyn.

"Bumpa too?"

Bumpa was what they had called Don.

To their astonishment, Brent and Donna had trouble sleeping that night. The Butts had put them in one twin-bedded room, and when they'd first seen the beds they'd exclaimed over how they would sleep the night away. But almost hourly, or so it seemed to them, one or the other would wake and turn on a light and want to talk.

"Sometimes I can't tell whether I'm asleep or not," Donna said, "and I just have to make sure I'm not dreaming and we're back at the plane."

"I know what you mean," Brent said.

Again and again, they talked of what they'd been through, and of their belief in God's influence on their survival.

"I wonder where our whiskey-jack is," Donna said.

The pain in her feet was, as had been predicted at Dr. Maxwell's clinic, devastating. Maxwell had given her a supply of pain-killers, but in spite of Brent's urging, she was reluctant to take more than the doctor had prescribed, and the throbbing made sleep even more difficult.

Donna Butts found them both awake at seven when she came to see if they were hungry.

"Hungry?" Brent said and, with Donna's assistance – Donna Johnson, that is; they laughed at the coincidence of their names – proceeded to order the largest breakfast either of their hosts could remember: juice, hot cereal, pancakes, poached eggs, toast and jelly and coffee for Brent, and, for Donna, orange juice, peaches, pancakes with whipped cream, strawberries and syrup, and tea. Neither of them was able to finish, but none of the dishes remained untouched.

More even than the food, they enjoyed washing the grime of the mountain from their bodies and hair. Donna went first. There was a tub in their bathroom, as she'd hoped, but she found the most efficient method was to stand in it, and use the overhead shower. She stayed there for over an hour, but still felt she hadn't cleansed herself thoroughly.

"It was black," she told Brent. "Not like normal dirt, just filthy black. I couldn't get *any* of it off back at Shirley's place, and it doesn't matter how much I scrub now there's still some left. My hands are still dirty, and I must have scrubbed them fifty times. But is it ever good just to feel the warm water running over you. I don't think I've got the tub clean."

She was right.

"I think you've left half the mountain in here," Brent called from the bathroom. "There's dead leaves in the bottom of the tub, and I think I can see fleas crawling around in them."

It took him twenty minutes to scrape the worst of the mess from the tub. Then he filled it with warm water for himself. While the water ran he shaved the stubble from his chin and cheeks. Tenderly, he lowered himself into the bath.

"There's no meat on my ass," he shouted through the wall.

"Stand up," Donna yelled back.

With a fingernail brush, he scrubbed his hands and wrists, and up his arms where, it seemed to him, the smoke from their fires had curled under his sleeves. He used the fingernail brush on his face, too, but it hurt, and he soaped up again and used a washcloth. His face took five soapings. Three times he rinsed his hair, and still the water ran dirty.

As he stood before the mirror, the thinness of his face and upper body shocked him. In spite of the number of pounds he'd lost, he wasn't aware until now of how thin he looked. He slipped into the clean underwear and fresh jeans the Butts had provided and went back into the bedroom.

"You look like a Biafran," Donna said. "Put a shirt on."

He finished dressing, and they sat down to await their families.

At seven that morning, a Cessna 206 from Air Unlimited in Challis and a National Guard helicopter that had been flown down from Boise the evening before had taken off to follow Brent's directions for locating the wreck of the plane. They found it quickly. The Cessna saw it first, although Loyd Todd, the pilot, and the two observers he'd taken with him all remarked they'd never have spotted its white carcass against the snow without Brent's map.

Loyd radioed the helicopter, flown by U.S. Air Force Colonel Roger Perkins, with a warrant officer, a crew chief, a CAP observer, and Sheriff Teuscher aboard. The helicopter landed on the ridge above the plane, and the entire party except Colonel Perkins made its way carefully down the hill. The tree that had evidently been hit by the plane's wing was still smouldering. Teuscher noticed a committee of Big Horn sheep on the mountainside to the plane's southeast, probably attracted by the helicopter's noise. Don's body was on the plane's rear seat. Teuscher and the others returned to the helicopter to fly back to Challis and organize a ground search for the missing pilot.

At 9:10, when the helicopter arrived at Challis, Teuscher went directly to the offices of Air Unlimited, the nerve centre of the airport. The flight building is a spacious, two-storey structure, walled, as is almost everything in Challis, with logs. Signs of aviation are everywhere: maps line the walls, the clock is set in the hub of a full-sized wooden propeller, and the radio spits and burps constantly in the work area. But it also reflects the special nature of the country it serves. The glass counter in front of the office houses a display of handguns. A sign in a window advertises hunting licences for sale. In the living quarters that open off the office, a bearskin rug is draped over the sofa. A man-sized dummy in cowboy clothes slouches in an armchair. In a glass case under a rock collection, a live rattlesnake watches the traffic come and go.

This morning, the building was a frenzy of activity. A reporter and photographer from the Boise *Daily Statesman* had driven down during the night, and they were waiting bleary-eyed for news. Other members of the press were starting to arrive. They joined Air Force and search and rescue personnel and a squadron of interested local pilots. Teuscher remained in command. He called Richard Maxwell at the clinic. Maxwell acts as coroner for Challis, and his permission was needed before Don's body could be moved. He gave it.

At 10:15, Boise Search and Rescue formally cancelled the ALNOT, the alert notice that had gone out nineteen days before.

At 11:30 an Air Force helicopter picked up the body and flew it to the Air Force base at Mountain Home, Idaho, and delivered it to the care of Verl Humphrey, funeral director and licenced coroner. The military questioned the necessity of moving it away from Challis. They were told to get in touch with Maxwell "right away," and, as the SAR log in Boise noted, "to give this call top priority."

The gathering press and radio were anxious for details. Sheriff Teuscher gave a brief statement about the welfare of the survivors and the location of the body. Dyer and Miss Johnson, he said, were not giving interviews at this time.

The search for Norm intensified. Aircraft not involved were asked to stay clear of the area. Helicopters circled the site. From Hailey, Idaho, capital of nearby Blaine County, Sheriff Ray Wheeler called to say he had a pack of search dogs ready to join in the hunt. Teuscher told him to stand by; a helicopter was despatched for the dogs. Teuscher moved some men up to Livingston Mine to prepare to set out on foot.

Shortly after noon, an Air Force helicopter dropped a team of four trained back-country mountaineers and paramedics on the ridge above the wreck of GYVP to try to trace the path Brent and Donna had described Norm as taking. They had difficulty moving through the heavy snow. Within half an hour, they could feel the sun beginning to scorch their faces.

At 12:45, Teuscher learned that a crew from KIFI, a television station in Idaho Falls, had arranged to charter a helicopter of their own and fly into the site to take pictures. Teuscher had one of the SAR men call their head office and explain as clearly and as bluntly as he could that the scene of the crash was off limits; the search had priority. Words about freedom of the press were exchanged. The chartered helicopter stayed on the ground.

Shortly after one o'clock, the paramedics from the search team began flashing sun-mirror signals to the circling aircraft. They had found Norm's body. It was less than half a mile downhill, but hidden by a bend in the canyon wall from the wreckage of his Skyhawk. The body was face up, as if resting in the snow. The wound in its temple was horribly evident. The laces of the shoes were still undone.

The paramedics signalled that their struggle with the deep snow had exhausted them. They would mark the location of the body and return the following day to remove it.

Mr. and Mrs. Robertson arrived in their motor home at the Village Inn just after one o'clock. Alerted by Brent and Donna, the Buttses quickly checked them into a room.

"But we're not telling anyone else where they are," Donna Butts informed the Robertsons. "There are an awful lot of press people around here. I even had to take Brent and Donna's lunch in to them hidden under a pile of clothes, so the reporters would think I was carrying laundry. They're awful pests. But the kids will be glad to see you."

In short order, the Robertsons became surrogate grandparents to the two young Canadians. When Donna declined an offer of soup, Mrs. Robertson brought forth a freshly baked carrot cake, which they found irresistible.

"Now you're not to worry about a thing," Mrs. Robertson said. "We've put your room in our name, and we'll stay with you till your real families get here." Donna's puppy was outside, she said.

"Can we see it?"

"Not unless you let us take some pictures of you," said Jimmy. "I want to remember *this* moment. Brent, take off your shirt."

"Do you really want to see how skinny I am?"

"Sure. This is something you'll never forget, and we want to share it with you."

They brought in the dog, as perfect as its picture, and Donna squealed with pleasure. And for the next few hours, the Robertsons gave them the most thoughtful gift of all: a chance to think about something other than their ordeal. Instead of asking, Mr. Robertson answered their questions, mostly about dog breeding, but when they wanted him to, he told them stories of his own boyhood, and Mrs. Robertson somehow found some more of her homemade carrot cake.

Chapter Sixteen

The Village Inn in Challis is actually three buildings: the office and the Butts' living quarters in one; guest quarters in the second, and, across a gravel courtyard, the restaurant. By the time the Johnson and Dyer families arrived from Estevan on Friday night, the scene resembled a battleground with the attacking forces – press and broadcasters – surrounding the defenders' last retreat.

The antagonism was also a symbolic one. To Brent and Donna, the world seemed to have divided itself into two camps: those who were with them and had their interests at heart – their relatives, the Robertsons, Tom and Donna Butts, and several of the authority figures, notably Sheriff Teuscher and Dr. Maxwell – on one side and everyone else – the professionally curious – on the other. There was no neutral ground. On Thursday night, Gary Doyle, an affable and competent young newsman at CJSL, the Estevan radio station that only the week before had donated much of its air time to raise money for the search, managed to get Brent on the line at the Inn. Brent's first reaction, he told Donna, had been to "ream him out," and only Doyle's assurance that he wanted to know only who was alive and who was dead had calmed him down.

With the arrival of their families, feelings between the protagonists of the story and the dozens of people who had descended on the scene to report it grew openly hostile. At one point, Jimmy Dyer, unmindful of his heart condition, launched a bodily attack on a crew from the commercial Canadian television network, CTV, with cries of "Punch them out, break their cameras!" Only after he'd been restrained did Jimmy notice that the weapon he had waved in challenge was a souvenir he had claimed for his own and intended to cherish: the walking stick Brent had used in his trek through the mountains.

There were a number of reasons for the tension. One was simple physical exhaustion on the part of not only the two young survivors, but also their families and the friends who had accompanied them to Challis. They had driven through the night and most of Friday to get there. After the emotional turmoil and the tears and hugs of their reunion, they were worn out. Their feelings were torn between the elation of knowing Brent and Donna had survived and the tragedy of the deaths. Sharon Pischke, for whom the news was bad, had stayed in Estevan, but those who travelled to Idaho had lost at the very least a friend or much admired acquaintance and, at the sorrowful most, a husband and a father. It was more than their nerves, tautened by the long wait of knowing nothing at all, could cope with. And with very few exceptions – Gary Doyle was one; Steve Anderson of the *Idaho Statesman*, who sent in a polite note to Brent and Donna, was another – the reporters on the scene paid little heed to what the principals in their story had been through.

Tact is not a common characteristic of the press, among whose members the Widow Brown syndrome – "Are you the Widow Brown?" "I'm *Mrs.* Brown," "Well, you're the Widow Brown now" – frequently flourishes. People whose daily trade involves digging into the details of everything from unexpected death to heroism can, and far too often do, forget that for the people whose lives they are digging into, these events are isolated and overpowering. Even to many veteran newsmen used to interviewing, those most closely involved with headline-making events, the wonder is not that their interviewees sometimes blow up at them, but that they don't do it far more often. Under stress, a surprising number of people forget their own right to privacy. It was perhaps not a coincidence that the man whose temper flared so publicly in the courtyard of the Inn was Jimmy Dyer, who in his years on the Estevan *Mercury* had seen the process through a reporter's eyes and was aware of his rights.

The professional sources in this case, moreover, were being strangely unco-operative. To a man they were unwilling to give more than the most basic facts; to any other questions, Teuscher, Maxwell, and the various SAR personnel replied, "No comment." The reporters would have to wait until the principals themselves decided to tell their stories.

On the other side, the families misunderstood the press as much as the press failed to sympathize with them. The stories that the reporters had written or broadcast almost daily through the search – and which they considered to be both accurate and helpful – had to the families at home been a constant offence against both their sensibility and their privacy. The flow of news – "Search Delayed By Poor Weather"; "Moods Range from Hope To Despair"; "Search Temporarily Abandoned" – and the persistent calls for information, had been a steady reminder of how public their private fears had become; they felt naked. Now, given a chance to face the representatives of the institutions they regarded as having added to their tribulations, they chose to snub them. The press had no more right to a share of their mingled joy and sorrow than it had had to pry into their terror.

There was, too, the matter of the cannibalism. Even within the compound of friends and family, there were two distinct groups: those who knew about it, and those who didn't. Sid Teuscher and Dr. Maxwell knew; Tom and Donna Butts did not. The paramedics who had picked up Don's body could not have failed to detect what had happened; Mr. and Mrs. Robertson, the grandparents *pro tem*, did not know. Most dramatically, Jimmy Dyer knew, and Brent told Cindy on Friday night when they were alone in their own room. Evelyn Johnson, the body of whose husband had sustained the life of their daughter, remained uninformed.

No conference was held, no interviews given. On Saturday evening, scarcely rested, the caravan of two cars and a van that had driven down from the Canadian prairie left Challis to go home.

In the days that followed, still unable to talk to the survivors themselves, the press continued to celebrate the triumph of Brent and Donna and to acknowledge Don's symbolic gift of the coat. Wire services spread the story around the world, and it was picked up and carried by papers as far away as Hong Kong.

Piece by piece, reporters were able to assemble the evidence. Somewhere outside Livingston, and almost certainly in the vicinity of

Burley, Norm had made a decision to fly directly over the mountains – from the handle of his route's sickle shape as straight as possible across to the tip of its blade. No record of a radio report of his decision was to be found, but reporters, working in concert with the SAR forces, were able to speculate that in the fading light he had made a bush pilot's gamble to go over the hump to Boise, and the storm had caught him unaware. They re-examined their maps. A straight edge placed between Livingston and Boise went directly across the point that was now known to represent the crash site. The mountain pilots shook their heads. No one, they believed, could have taken that route deliberately. It was beyond their comprehension. Even so, the lines of two route searches came tantalizingly close to the crash location; they could very well have missed it by flying the wrong side of a peak.

Among professionals and perhaps even more among the amateurs who had laboured so heroically on the search there were dozens of "if onlys." If only the plane had been orange.... If they'd had a giant balloon on board, one that could be inflated and sent aloft on a thousand-foot string.... If only they'd had an emergency locator ...or, most of all, filed a flight plan.... If only, that is, it had been stuck to.

From Laurel, Richard Hatfield called to see how close Clyde Praye had been. The spot Clyde had drawn on the map of Salmon River was eighteen miles from the downed Cessna. Two towers? Well, yes, as a matter of fact, there were two fire towers not far from the site. But there were fire towers throughout the mountains. Second-guessing was much easier now that people knew where the Skyhawk had been.

The newspapers continued to publish as many details as they could round up. Reporters drove up the difficult road to the Livingston Mine to interview Elmer and Shirley Swanson; they talked with the people who'd brought the bodies out. But the consumption of Don's flesh remained private. "They ate weeds, grass ... anything they could," Elmer Swanson told the Regina *Leader-Post*. Ron Dunagan, one of the paramedics who'd gone in to the site on Friday, told the *Idaho Statesman* that he was "concentrating too much on removing the body to observe what the young couple had eaten."

Privately, there was speculation. As early as Sunday morning, when he arrived back in Boise from his vigil in Challis, Rich Mauer of the *Statesman* was asked by his wife, "Well, did they eat him?" And others, spurred by the continued reluctance of Brent and Donna to offer full disclosure, wondered whether the plane had been carrying illegal drugs, or whether the two young people had had sex. None of the rumours saw print. An attempt by the *National Enquirer*, a scandal-hungry tabloid published out of Florida, to buy juicy details was rebuffed.

There is, on reflection, reason to believe that some of the reporters who followed the story knew of the cannibalism but decided, out of concern for the families, not to publish what they knew. None of them will admit it, however. News people do not readily admit to holding back on stories, particularly when their motive is decency. In the news business, kindness can be taken too easily for a weakness of will.

Norm Pischke was buried in a private service on Tuesday, May 29. The following day, at two in the afternoon, services were held at St. John the Baptist Roman Catholic Church in Estevan for Don Johnson. The casket was closed. That day's edition of the *Leader-Post* carried an editorial honouring Brent and Donna. "There's a lesson for all of us in their story," said its anonymous author. "It is that the human spirit can often triumph in even the most unlikely circumstances. And it is somehow reassuring that the central players in this drama of endurance were two young people."

On its six o'clock news that same night, KTVB in Boise broadcast the news that Don's body had been cannibalized. The newscast cited, but did not name, "two reliable sources." Who those sources were remains a mystery. Phil Wendstrand and Sal Celeski, two KTVB reporters who often worked as a team, and who wrote the story for the station, have steadfastly refused to identify them. The sources were not any of the people who had closed ranks with the family in Challis. Neither Sid Teuscher nor Richard Maxwell would even confirm the accuracy of the report after it was published; both continued to stick by their principles of "no comment." Dr. Maxwell, in fact, called the publication of the news "disgusting" and "an invasion of privacy."

"It's toying with the mental health of the two people involved," he was to say later, "when people should have been jumping up and down on their Bibles and saying 'hallelujah, they're alive.'" But by this time the list of people who had either seen Don's body in transit or who could have talked to someone who might even have been standing in Maxwell's office when Brent and Donna were first reporting what they had done was a long one, and any of a couple of dozen people could have had a friend in the press.

At no time up to the revelation had either Brent or Donna, or any of the people closest to them, lied about the consumption of the flesh. Nor were they ashamed of what they had done. They were, as they have remained, certain of the rectitude of their action. In their own hearts they had done no wrong; and without exception, the people to whom they did relate their decision, from Sheriff Teuscher on the bumpy road down from the Swansons to the Reverend Robert Wadey, the Johnsons' parish priest, told them they had been morally right.

What was developing, in fact, was a phenomenon that continued to be evident throughout the dissemination of the news: people who heard about it felt *they* themselves understood, but they were often worried about what *others* might say. The "others" were never named; they were simply people who would be less understanding of the realities of the case. The principle was not unlike that which governs censorship, where, for example, a group of "experts" can sit through hours of a film dealing with explicit sex and reason that although *they* will emerge unscathed from the experience it will drive "others" to commit heinous deeds.

Brent and Donna, moreover, had not been asked about cannibalism. Whether they would have chosen to keep their silence if the Boise television station had not blurted out the news that evening will never be known. When it happened, their long-term intentions were less important than their immediate concern.

Whatever their motives for not reporting a story – decency, kindness, laziness, or ignorance – members of the free North American press are prepared to keep the secret only so long as all other members keep it. Once any part of the media has carried the story, others react. This system gives us both the best and worst of free journalism.

When the *Washington Post* detects a Watergate, other members of the fourth estate follow suit, often, in their chagrin at being beaten to the first disclosure, working even harder in their follow-ups. But when, similarly, one part of the system reveals, or even alleges, the "facts" of a story whose publication can serve no public good and conceivably do irretrievable personal harm, other parts of the system jump blindly into the fray, and the public becomes aware, if sometimes only through subsequent denial, of a private affair, a personal secret.

When the Boise television station broke the story that Wednesday night, the phones in Estevan began to ring. Had they or hadn't they?

And until that moment, the most important person in the world to Brent and Donna – Evelyn Johnson – did not know.

Evelyn was their first concern. She must not read what had happened to her husband's body until they had told her themselves.

After the funeral, the family gathered at what even then they were calling Evelyn's house, as it had been Don's house before. Father Wadey asked Evelyn to join him and Brent and Brian in private. They retired upstairs. Donna remained in the living room with the rest of the mourners. Speaking quietly, Father Wadey told her what had happened on the mountain, while Brent looked steadily on. She returned his gaze. There was a moment's silence. Evelyn spoke to Brent.

"You did what was right," she said. "It's what Don would have wanted you to do. He would have been very proud of you both."

As much perhaps as it ever will, life returned to normal for Brent and Donna over the next several months. Their physical wounds began to heal. In a wheelchair, Donna emerged from her seclusion shortly after her father's funeral to receive from her school a letter for her achievements as a majorette and a standing ovation from her contemporaries. Her teachers decided to allow her to graduate with the marks she had gained at the Christmas exams, and she has since applied some of her business acumen to a growing involvement in the family business, now run by Evelyn and Brian, who reminds more and more people of Don. With therapy, she regained her ability to walk easily, and at summer's end, with her skin bronzed by the prairie sun, she was once again playing tennis with Ron Coulter, whom she plans to marry. Her dog, the West Highland White Terrier, is her constant companion. She calls it Boise.

The scar under Brent's chin is still visible and may mark him for life, but his teeth have been replaced by a denture he finds uncomfortable but useful. His own teeth were placed under Geoffrey's pillow one night, and in the morning Geoffrey found a crisp twenty dollar bill where they had been. Before the hunting season had arrived, Brent was scampering about his job and his pleasures without even the limp that had been noticeable for much of the summer. The patio has been carpeted, as neatly as he promised, and his happiest moments are now spent tending the hedge around the yard on Nicholson Road, or spinning about town in his purple dune buggy. Although there have been occasional difficulties in moving licence plates back and forth, he still prefers the dune buggy to the maroon Thunderbird Jimmy gave him on his return.

Psychologically, who knows? For a time when he returned, Brent had some trouble sleeping and would often want to spend nights outdoors. But he had never slept well before. Donna has reported no dreams of being on the mountain. Both talk easily of their experience, with a frankness that sometimes embarrasses their listeners, who often tend to be less direct than Brent and Donna themselves are. Self-conscious visitors will sometimes find themselves groping for euphemisms for cannibalism, or trying to avoid figures of speech that may seem to have unfortunate ramifications. To Brent and Donna, what they did was to eat parts of Don. That is a part of their story. There are other parts too. Only by listening to them carefully can one learn how comfortable with their actions they truly are.

It is the same with the religious experience that moved them so deeply. Neither has become a proselytizing Christian. They feel no need to convince anyone else that God brought them out of the valley of the shadow of death. They know He did. It is enough for them. It is true.

There have been remarks. Among those segments of the media that have written or broadcast with the greatest sensitivity, some people have made private jokes that break the boundaries of taste. At one

Regina radio station a technician helping to record the news of Brent and Donna's heroic escape said off the air to his announcer: "I'd have walked out of there too, rather than be eaten." But the important aspect of this kind of comment has been its rarity. The townspeople of Estevan have not only accepted and understood what the two young people did on the mountainside, they have applauded them for it; in the pubs and curling leagues of Estevan, Brent and Donna are heroes; and in more than one family where parents have discussed the case with their children, the parents have said that under similar circumstances – God forbid – they hoped their children would do the same thing.

When, on May 30, it became inevitable that they deal publicly with the facts of the cannibalism, Brent and Donna were served extraordinarily well by their lawyers, who, in accordance with the wishes of the Johnsons and the Dyers, were handling the affair. The lawyers called a news conference, but with unusual perspicacity, they asked the three members of the Saskatchewan media who were invited – Gary Doyle of CJSL; Peter Ng, the publisher of the Estevan *Mercury*, and Wilf Chabun, a reporter from the Regina *Leader-Post* for whose reliability the paper's editor was prepared to vouch – to agree, as a condition of being able to write the story, that they submit their manuscripts for approval before releasing them. Doyle, Ng, and Chabun went along.

The press conference was emotional. Brent, who willingly answered all questions, broke into tears as he recalled some of the grimmest moments on the mountain. The stories were written with remarkable perspective. Chabun, a thorough reporter and vivid writer, wrote thirty-five paragraphs before he typed: "Only when their food was virtually gone, did they decide to eat from Johnson's body." The lawyers suggested that a more accurate version would delete the word "virtually," and change "eat" to read "consume some of the flesh of." It was their only change. Chabun readily agreed to its accuracy. His story became the basis for news reports across the continent and around the world.

The money that was raised to pursue the search for Brent and Donna has become a special fund, administered by many of the people who helped to raise it, including the young broadcasters Brent

Johner and Kathy Muirhead. It makes money available to other families in other communities who might face similar crises. Part of it has also been set aside to contribute to the education of the Pischke children.

Evelyn Johnson carries on, looking forward to more grandchildren. Sharon Pischke runs Norm Air, and tries not to look up too expectantly when she hears the sound of a Cessna coming in to land.

Business flourishes at Dyer Ford, where Jimmy continues to blister bureaucrats, and quietly to make sure that the troubled young man he promised to hire stays on the path of sobriety for which Brent remains his best example.

In June of 1979, in a quiet ceremony at St. John the Baptist Church, Brent and Cindy Dyer were remarried in the Catholic faith. After the ceremony, Cindy laid her bridal bouquet of lilacs on her father's grave.

Acknowledgements

Brent Dyer and Donna Johnson, whose story this is, are remarkable reporters as well as remarkable human beings. The accuracy of their memories must have added to the pain of many of the moments from the spring of 1979 as they relived them with me. I am grateful to them, as I am to members of their families who had to relive their own anguish. I thank also the less conspicuous participants in the story who shared their experiences; many of their names appear in the narrative, but there were others. Only one person, Sharon Pischke, wished to retain her own privacy and that of her children. I respect her decision. The passages on her premonitions and on the early years of her life with Norm have been freely discussed with me and with others. Dennis and Vera Ball were inordinately kind to me during my stay in a part of the world I first knew as a newspaperman twenty years ago, as were so many people in Estevan. Marcia Kirscher provided me with invaluable technical research. Jan Walter watched the manuscript evolve and offered suggestions and support. Ken Lefolii gave it what at *Maclean's* magazine we used to call a "read." I thank also Jennifer Glossop, in Toronto, and Judith Kern, in New York. Brent and Donna have asked that *The Sacrament* be dedicated to the memory of Don Johnson, and I happily oblige.